Endorsements

My spirit was not only stirred up to worship, but I was also deeply enlightened on what worship is. Every worshiper needs this teaching and motivation. Biblical worship is not only in words, but in actions. Worship brings God back to the gospel and the church. Welcome to the worship workshop.

—Pastor D Tindike (Lecturer,
Heritage of Faith Bible Institute, Soweto)

This book is so anointed. It is always natural for anyone to relate to personal experiences; that's what makes this book outstanding.

—Pastor Baldwin Baloyi (founder and
presiding pastor of Life of God Ministry)

TOTAL WORSHIP

A Life of Deep Communion with God

LUCKY L. SELEPE

WESTBOW®
PRESS
A DIVISION OF THOMAS NELSON
& ZONDERVAN

WestBow Press books may be ordered through booksellers or by contacting:

WestBow Press
A Division of Thomas Nelson & Zondervan
1663 Liberty Drive
Bloomington, IN 47403
www.westbowpress.com
1 (866) 928-1240

ISBN: 978-1-4908-7085-4 (sc)
ISBN: 978-1-4908-7083-0 (hc)
ISBN: 978-1-4908-7084-7 (e)

Library of Congress Control Number: 2015903272

Print information available on the last page.

WestBow Press rev. date: 02/19/2015

Contents

Acknowledgments

First of all, let me acknowledge my God, Jehovah, for giving me the privilege to put these revelations and inspirations in a book format. I have never been a natural writer. Therefore, putting this material together is a miracle of His grace. The truths in this book are not the product of the natural man; they are God at work, and I believe that those who read will receive from the throne room of glory and partake of the same abundant grace.

I want to acknowledge and appreciate my lovely wife, Rose Selepe, who had to sacrifice time and encouraged me to write this book to the glory of God. Without her support, this work would not be possible.

Also, I would love to acknowledge the contributions of Pastor Kagiso Mthembu (also known as KG) and Pastor Stephen Selepe. I deeply appreciate my lecturer, Pastor Tindike, who sacrificed His time to proofread and gave me valuable input for this project. The same goes to pastor Baldwin Baloyi and Pastor Steven Selepe, who took time to proofread the manuscript.

Preface

When one has many life-changing experiences with God, he or she has no choice but to share it with the body of Christ. *Total Worship: The Life of Deep Communion With God* is a divine inspiration from God, based on practical encounters with God through worship. I have come to a point where I cannot afford to ignore the burden and inspiration of putting such a treasure of experiences in writing. I had to ask God for the grace to be able to write. I am highly confident that many will be inspired to experience God through the power of biblical worship.

Introduction

> But the hour is coming, and now is, when the true worshipers will worship the Father in spirit and in truth; for the father is seeking such to worship Him.
>
> —John 4:23

Though often misconstrued, worship remains the most integral and fundamental element of our relationship with God. The greatest of all Christian experiences is that of deep communion with God/Jehovah. Everything else follows this kind of relationship. The deepest level of communion with God is arrived at through true biblical worship. The essence of Christianity hinges around worship. The Church of Christ cannot exist at all without worship.

Jesus showed the Samaritan woman that the people had been worshipping incorrectly. One of the reasons was that they had been worshipping a god they didn't know. This meant that people could genuinely go about worshipping God, only to find that they were doing it incorrectly. Then what is true worship? And how do we worship God the right way? It seems that one could commit one's whole life to something that is not true worship. That would be indeed a real failure of life.

When I received a revelation of what true worship is, I discovered that I had been missing out all along. The challenge is often that we do not know that we are missing out; thus we neither push any further nor even strive for another level. It seems almost impossible for one to get enough of worship, once one gets a true revelation of God regarding worship. Worship can be addictive. The more you know about worship, the more you develop an insatiable desire to know and worship Him more, and the more effective you become in worship. The more one worships, the hungrier one gets for worship.

Visions about Worship

One night, I was praying to and worshipping God. I laid myself across the floor in surrender to the Most High God. I was groaning in the spirit. I was in deep fellowship with Him. My spirit was in union with the Spirit of God, declaring the deep things of God. As soon as I was satisfied, I went to sleep, and that's when I saw a vision.

In the vision, I saw myself lying prostrate across the floor, worshipping God. I heard a whispering voice that affirmed me, saying, "This is the way to worship." In the spirit I saw a wave of power and glory stirred up and filling the church. Then God revealed to my spirit that if I want to see the power and the glory of God, I must be a true worshiper. This led me to want to understand what true worship is all about. God was leading me to something that would change the atmosphere of worship in the church.

The Bible says that they that worship must worship in spirit and in truth. (See John 4: 23.) I had to know what it meant to worship in truth and in spirit. God started dealing with me in this area, and He attested to it with signs.

The Vision: Jesus Christ Manifests in Response to Worship

The first confirmation was a vision God gave to one of our pastors, by the name of Kagiso (also known as KG). In the vision, according to his report, a few members of our church were going up a mountain as a group. All of a sudden it was only me and him at the apex of the mountain. Immediately I said to Him, "KG, let's bow down and worship, for I can sense the glory of God." Upon bowing down, we saw fire from a distance, and out of it came Jesus. He then came straight toward us.

This vision meant that if we truly worship God and are sensitive to His presence, then we shall see God. This prompted us to start practicing the respect of His presence. This led to a second confirmation, which involved practical manifestations of the power of God.

One night while in overnight prayer, I asked everyone to keep quiet to respect the presence of the Holy Spirit. While quiet like that, with our eyes closed, people started falling down from their seats. I knew it was not me, because I had never considered this; I hadn't intended to make these people fall. I was genuinely respecting the presence of God, in the Holy Spirit, by faith. He was in essence confirming His presence as we acted in faith. It was an obvious manifestation of what God was doing among us. God's presence was manifesting in our midst. People started deeply groaning from their spirits unto God, prostrating across the floor. For more than an hour people were prostrate on the floor, not petitioning anything to God, but glorifying Him in the Spirit.

Another time, we were singing worship songs and I laid myself prostrate across the floor. While I was worshipping, people started falling from their feet. Oh, what a glorious night! Their feet could not carry them because of the *kavod*—the heaviness of the presence of God. Worship indeed reveals and manifests the glory of God. If the church has to experience God, true worship must be restored back to the church.

CHAPTER 1

The God of the Universe

For since the creation of the world His invisible attributes are clearly seen, being understood by the things that are made, even His eternal power and Godhead, so that men are without excuse.

—Romans 1:20

Critical defining moments of our faith often occur during times of great discomfort. That's when we get out of our comfort zones and use more effort in order to change situations at hand. Though it does not necessarily have to be like that, situations compel us to push our bounds in prayer and faith, seeking God more. However, to the body of Christ this should not be the case. Consistent and deep fellowship with God must be a natural phenomenon to a recreated man. We should not seek God because of problems. Of course, problems will always come; but when they do, we are always ready to celebrate our victory. Nevertheless, this was the case with me. I was still a baby in the knowledge of God. Though I had been born again two years earlier and was committed to prayer and fasting, the idea of intimacy with God still evaded me significantly. I trusted God to deal with my troubles, yet did not know there is a better way. And I am convinced it is the case with many in the body of Christ now. Yet it was in perilous times that I had an amazing encounter with God when I knew Him as the El Olam (God of the Universe).

My Critical Times

I will always remember how God changed my life through worship. Most fundamental for us as believers, if we want to be able to get out of situations victoriously, is the revelation that will develop concrete living faith in our spirits. This time God revealed himself to me and I saw the power of worship. It was in the year 2000 that something remarkable that transformed my spiritual life happened. I was studying toward an honors degree in social sciences and had a lot of stressful challenges.

It is important to note that by then my family was facing financial constraints, which to a large extent affected my studies and emotions. I would go home and find that we didn't even have toothpaste. That's how bad the situation was. Have you ever regretted being born in your family? *I had a poor heritage,* I thought to myself. I was not yet aware of the heritage I have in Christ. This affected me such that sometimes I had to depend on handouts. At times I would see other students drinking alcohol, and I would think to myself, *for each beer they drink, I could buy bread and survive for a day or two.* They were fortunate and had money to waste on alcohol. Yet some of us have gone around not knowing where to get the next meal, having to study at the same time to chase the dream of a better future. It was at this point that I almost had emotional breakdown. I even had to seek psychological intervention, but when I came out of each session, I felt that I needed something more than empathy and more powerful than human effort. Indeed, I needed a miracle worker. I was in a place where I knew I had too much for a human to carry.

Most importantly, I could not afford to buy any study materials. This had been my experience since my first year at the university. My classmates could afford to buy books. When given an assignment, I still had to compete with them for the few available reference resources in the library. Unfortunately for me, most of the time, I would find that they had already been taken when I got there. I had to wait for them to finish their assignments, and then I would start mine. At times some would lend me study materials on the condition that I would teach them what I learned and share my notes. It was a norm for me to work against time because of these constraints.

One time, after a lot of struggle, I managed to draft my assignment with just a few days left. I went to the computer lab to type the assignment. When nearing the end, the assignment just disappeared, and I was told this happened because of a vicious virus. It happened the first time and the second time, and I didn't complain. On the day before the due date, it happened again, and it was late in the afternoon. I got out of that lab and I said to God, "Now I am tired." My neck was stiff and tight with cramps, and I had a mild headache. I saw blackness before me. My hope was waning. I even discovered that I had heart palpitations.

I felt that it was not fair. I was the only one born again in my class, but it seemed that I had to work even harder than every one of them, for only meager results. I had to put in more effort than all of them. I felt it was God's fault, because obviously I was doing my best. Why couldn't He protect my interests? If He really loved and cared for me, why was He not protecting me against the sabotage of the Enemy? If He was the all knowing, the all-sufficient, the all-powerful, why didn't He do something about it? Those who were not born again had it easier than I did. So I started questioning the authenticity of the Word. All the promises that we "shall be the head and not tails," seemed to be only motivation with a placebo effect. It seemed that it was only meant to make us feel good for a moment, without real, life-changing substance. I was ready now to question God. I cried tears, imagining what would happen to me if I failed. I went to 1800 prayer and came back to student residence still bitter. However, that night, though very tired, I could not catch even a little sleep. Eventually I had to take an unusual step, which determined the events that were to follow.

My Defining Moment

At 0000 I decided to wake up. I went to pray on the concrete roof of the building. I didn't want to wake my cousin up, as I was sharing my room with him. I was ready to complain to God again when I raised my hand and looked up to address God, who was supposedly in heaven. Immediately I cast my eyes on the full moon and the stars. In a split second my soul was illuminated by the divine truth of what I was seeing. I imagined that the moon was in space and nothing physical was holding it in its place. The same was true of the stars, the sun, and all other planets that are known and unknown.

Instead of complaining, I said, "God, I thank you. Now I understand that what they call gravity is your power. You hold the moon and the stars in your hands. The sun never collides with the moon or with the earth I am standing on. This is your power. If you can hold the moon and the stars and the earth and the sun in their places, then you can hold my very life. Oh, God, I believe now that I will graduate, because I will pass this year."

Lightning from the Sky

While I was praying like that, the bitterness, resentment, worry, and fear disappeared. For the first time, I prayed in other tongues, and unexplainable groaning flooded out of my spirit. My heart was overflowing with unspeakable joy, and tears flooded my cheeks. Suddenly a bolt of lightning flashed from the sky. I said to God, "I don't understand, but I believe that you will make me understand." That night I went to sleep as if nothing were wrong. Down in my spirit I knew all was well. I didn't know how it was going to happen. I thought God would worry about that.

The following day, my deadline was about 1500, and still I didn't have my assignment ready, yet joy filled my soul.

In the morning I woke up in the same mood, attended classes, and went for 1300 prayer, still without my assignment. I didn't ask God anything that day; neither did I try to rebuke the Devil. I continued from where I had left off the previous night—telling God how big He is, and that He holds all things, including the earth I was standing on, by the word of His power. (See Hebrews 1:3.)

Satan Is Subjected under My Feet (Lightning Explained)

While praising and worshipping, the Spirit of God illuminated my soul. He said that the lightning I saw was how the Enemy fell and that it was a Scripture. At the time, I did not know where the Scripture was; only later did I find out that it is Luke 10:18: "I saw satan fall like a lightning from heaven." I thought to myself, *If the Devil fell that hard, it means he is still lying on his belly, groaning in pain. So he is still under my feet.* I started thanking God for subjecting the Enemy under my feet. Now that was something to shout about. I understood I had a reason to celebrate God. I knew from then that I was not forsaken all along. I just needed to tap into the mode of God. Worship lifted me into that divine mode. I believe the angels had to join me in this.

The Authority of Worship

Worship is our battle cry. It provokes God of the armies of Israel to get into the forefront of the battle lines. While I was worshipping God, He was at work on my behalf. When I left that prayer session, I went straight to the computer lab. I was led to go straight to all the computers I had used previously. Then I started searching for the work I had saved on each computer. Miraculously, all the documents had been restored on all the computers. I just consolidated all the work, edited it, and printed it. By 1500 (the last hour before the deadline) I was able to submit my complete assignment with other students. I had no more stress, no more ulcers, no headache, and no stiff neck. I was wholly restored, but even more, my doubts were totally smitten. More importantly, I had just discovered a key to move mountains, which is worship. Worship authorizes God to start working on your behalf.

From then my prayer changed. Instead of asking God, I would just soak myself in worship, making declarations of the things I wanted to see happening. For example, whenever I faced the same problem with impossible deadlines, I would postpone the class from the spirit realm, through worship and declarations, and it would practically manifest. I would hide under a desk and say, "My God you are so big and sovereign. You need no help from anyone. You are bigger than my lecturer. I thank you because the lecturer is not coming to class tomorrow for my sake." What would happen the following day would be amazing; the lecturer would briefly appear and say, "Morning class! Please receive my apologies, something urgent came up. Please finish up your assignments and submit tomorrow." I would not be surprised, because I knew how it happened. Praise God! He is the God of all flesh, and nothing is impossible with Him. He is big, and He is my universe. He is the Lord my redeemer, who would make other nations ransoms for a believer. (See Isaiah 43:3.)

God of the Universe Declared through His Creation

We look at the universe and know God created it. Scientists operate only on the known and naturally observable universe. I have full confidence that there is more of it that is not yet known. Yet based on the little we can observe, the Scripture says, "… His invisible attributes are clearly seen, being understood by the things that are made, even His eternal power and Godhead, so that they are without excuse" (Romans 1:20). Yet the Creator is greater than the creation. When you look at the creation, you can really get a glimpse of the revelation of God. He is God of the universe. I understand that the universe is without ends or edges. The planets exist in a vast and infinite space that cannot be measured. Yet He is the one who created it. And the Bible says, "He fills all things" (Ephesians 1:22). He fills the universe. God can't be measured in size, in time, or in any other way. The universe is in Him, and humanly speaking, it has no end. And the Bible says that men have no excuse for not worshipping Him. But instead of worshipping the immortal God, they worship images made to look like mortals or birds or animals or reptiles. (See Romans 1:23 GNT.)

Think of the sun, which no human device can dare get to. Anything that approached it would dematerialize beyond recognition because of the extreme heat it gives off. Yet the bible says He fills all things, which includes the sun. God fills the sun, and He is immune to that heat. He himself is the consuming fire (Hebrews 12:29). God can consume the fire Himself. Heaven and earth will pass away, but God is eternal.

King David had the following revelation: "The **heavens declare the glory of God; and the firmament sheweth His handiwork.** Day unto day uttereth speech, and night unto night sheweth knowledge. There is no speech nor language, where their voice is not heard. Their line is gone out through all the earth and their words to the end of the world" (Psalm 19:1–4 KJV).

The word *firmament* refers to the vast space in which all the known and unknown planets are set. It seems that the works of God have the same effect as His Word. The creations tell a story—a testimony of the attributes of God that is able to lead man into the revelation of God. The creation is a testimony that is able to conceive faith unto salvation. When we observe the creation, it must give us the motivation to seek and know the Creator. All these things tell of the greatness and the deity of our God. They tell us that He is worthy to be worshipped and to be praised.

God of All Flesh

If God is the God of the universe, He therefore owns everything in it. However, in the entire vast universe, man is His most treasured possession. He created man and gave him dominion over all His creation. Man directly belongs and accounts to God, the Creator. God declares that He is the God of all flesh. (See Jeremiah 32:27.) Whether we acknowledge Him or not, He is God over all flesh. All flesh must worship Him. He has power over all flesh. Irrespective of our status in society, we are accountable to God. He removes kings and raises up kings (See Daniel 2:21.) Our worship means everything to Him. He created us for His own pleasure. As such, we are to please God.

CHAPTER 2

Designed to Worship

In the beginning, God created man in His own image and in His own likeness. (See Genesis 1:27.) Why? For man to have total fellowship with Him. Thus, embedded deep in the heart of man is an insatiable desire to worship God. Even before the foundations of the earth, man was designed and wired in his fibers to be a worshipper. Man has an innate and irresistible urge to worship engraved in his spirit. The need to worship is universal, irrespective of culture, race, or creed.

Adam was naturally created to worship, glorify, and honor God wholly. There was a perfect fellowship between God and man until sin interfered. There was a complete union between God and man through eternal life. God would come to the garden and fellowship with the couple. But because of Adam's treason, the perfection of fellowship was broken. The union was broken. He lost eternal life. That eternal life was and still is in Christ. See what the Scripture says: "And we know that the Son of God has come, and has given us understanding so that we can know the true God. And now we live in fellowship with the true God, because we have fellowship with His son, Jesus Christ. He is the only true God, **and He is eternal life**" (1 John 5:20; see also Isaiah 9:6).

Eternal life is a person. God is that eternal life. That's what or who Adam lost. Adam's treason cost him Jesus. Jesus was in Adam as the word and Spirit. There is a void in men that can be satiated only by serving (worshipping) the almighty God in Christ Jesus. The greatest calamity, therefore, is missing who the right God is, thus worshipping other gods.

The Devil, taking advantage, swayed people's minds, capitalizing on that innate desire within man to worship for his own plans. Yet he is just an angel also created by God. In the hierarchy of God's kingdom, the Enemy is below man. Yet when one bows to the Enemy (Lucifer), it means that one is really going lower. He has created nothing. He is himself a creation, just like you. He was posted as Lucifer, worshipping God, until he fell to pride. Now he wants man to do the same, because he knows his time is short.

All the energy and hunger for worshipping God was thereafter rechanneled to wrong things so man would always be turned against God and not worship Him. Instead man started religion. Hence there are so many religions today, all of them with the sole purpose of subjecting lives to different objects of worship. Unfortunately, as long as one is not worshipping Jehovah, it means that one is worshipping a created object. Some worship the stars, some the moon, the sun, animals, people, worlds, rivers, and seas, to mention but a few.

Some, though they knew that they had to worship Jehovah, created man-made systems and traditions without revelation and substance of the Spirit, coming up with religion instead, and they called it Christianity. He was right when He said they would come in His name. (See Matthew 24:5.) Some of these have been turned into different religious cults and other evil practices. All of this happens because of the irresistible innate hunger for worship.

Only worshipping the one true God in the right way can fill the void in the heart of man. There is a way to quench the spiritual hunger. We need to know how God has positioned and prioritized worship from the beginning, in order to understand the best way to worship God. God wants to be the only object of worship. Remember that He said, "You shall have no other gods before me. You shall make yourself a carved image, or any likeness of anything that is in heaven above, or that is in the earth beneath, or that is in the water under the earth. You shall not bow down to them or serve them, for I the Lord your God am jealous God" (Exodus 20:1–10).

We need to understand what effective worship can do among the body of Christ. This book, which is a revelation of Jesus on how to get God, was manifested through the power of effective biblical worship. God gave us the revelation about worship through visions, studying the Word, and practical manifestations. God changed the atmosphere of worship in the church such that we now see worship for what it truly is.

Whether one knows it or not—whether or not one is conscious or unconscious of this fact—man is a natural worshipper. Hence man will always find something to worship, such that if need be, he can create something right now and bow to it for to worship. God is the first and the last. He is the Alpha and the Omega. He is the Creator of all things, and He is the one and only one to bow to. Our lives must be committed to the Creator of all things. We must channel our drives and energies to worship Jehovah instead of other things. "Dear children, keep away from anything that might take God's place in your heart" (1 John 5:21 NLT).

CHAPTER 3

What Is Worship?

We have often confined worship to a Sunday service, especially the time dedicated to singing. When we look into the Holy Scriptures, we find that there is more to worship than singing and praising. Worship is broader, deeper, and more powerful than that. It is not only necessary but also compulsory for the life of a Christian. It is one of the best ways to resist the Enemy. It would, however, be impossible for one to maintain or even enter the life and essence of worship unless one knew what true biblical worship is. We have often worshipped amiss, not understanding what worship means.

Worship is a greater dimension of fellowship with God. It is a life wholly given to God, even unto death. (See Revelation 12:11). This means total surrender unto God, in acknowledgment that He is God. It is more than a song or a mere act or words. We will focus on two major contexts of worship: the life of worship and acts of worship.

Worship as Fellowship[1]

Christianity is a restored relationship with God. Jesus came to

---
[1]   See more in chapter 5

restore perfection in fellowship with God. Our relationship is manifold. We fellowship with God, putting on manifold hats as Christians. The church puts on the hat of the bride, and He the groom; the church, sons, and He, Father; the church, servants, and He the Lord. In fellowship we recognize and express God's Lordship, fatherhood, and everything else He is to us. The deepest or even highest level of fellowship is attained through worship. The word *fellowship* is synonymous with "communion." It suggests a picture of people in a close or intimate relationship, sharing and exchanging. It is a reciprocal communication between man and God. We are tied together with God in the bond of love.

Worship as Ministering or Serving

The word *worship* is often interchangeable with the word *serve*. The Hebrew word often translated to "worship" is *"abad,"* which generally means "to serve or work." But in this context it implies "to work as a slave" or "to serve." This means that one recognizes that he or she is being owned by God. Unlike human masters, our master is a just, righteous, gracious, and compassionate one. Thus we are the slaves of righteousness; we are slaves to His grace and the redemptive works of God in Christ. It is in the same context as ministering, just as when the disciples ministered to God in Acts 13:2. Generally, when ministering unto God we do not petition or ask for anything selfish from our God, but we wait on Him. We arouse God's pleasure and satisfaction. Paul and other apostles often introduced themselves in their epistles as servants (or bondservants). In Romans 1:1, for example, Paul wrote, "Paul, a bond servant of Jesus Christ, Called to be an apostle, separated to the Gospel of God ..."

Total Surrender

Another important Hebrew word for worship is *shachah* or *sagad*, which means "to depress or prostrate oneself in a way humbling oneself to the one who is considered greater." This is complete humility to honor the supremacy of the Almighty. In the book of Luke 5:12, we hear of a man with leprosy who came and fell facedown and begged Jesus to heal him. The word for "falling down" is also translated as "worship." For example, in the same incident, Matthew 8:2 puts it in context as follows: "And behold, a leper came and worshiped Him, saying, 'Lord, if you are willing, you can make me clean.'"

Acts of Worship[2]

There are things we do to express and declare our worship to God. These I would love to call acts of worship. These acts mean nothing to God unless they express our heart's reverence, gratitude, love, submission, and so on.

Total Worship

Total worship therefore focuses on two levels of worship. The first level is total surrender and affection of the heart. The second level is how we express our heartfelt unconditional surrender and affection to God, and we will call this the act of worship. The two words *serve* and *humble*, in the context of worship, are a powerful combination. The life of worship is when your whole life is totally yielded (hence the word *humble* or *prostrate*) to serve God in all conditions, at all times. The act of worship is therefore the expression of one's submissiveness to God.

Just as the Bible says you shall not serve other gods (see Exodus 34:14), total surrender is special and exclusive submission unto God. In this context it means you shall not worship other gods. Another good example is Joshua 24:15. Joshua said, *"And if it seems evil for you to* **serve** the Lord, choose for yourselves this day whom you will **serve**, whether the gods which your fathers **served** that were on the other side of the river or the Gods of the Amorites, in whose land you dwell. But as for me and my house, we will **serve** the Lord."

In some translations, such as *The New Century Version* (NCV), the word *serve*, in our reference Scripture, is translated as "worship." In this context it means, "yield your life to God for worship." It is not just an

---

[2]   See chapter 5 for various examples.

act; rather, it is a lifelong commitment to serve God just because He is God.

The one who serves is called a servant. In the Bible, servanthood has a connotation of slavery. You assume the position of a slave and God becomes your supreme Lord and master. A servant in this case has no personal vision, choice, or independence. You do what your master says ought to be done. You yield to the directions and instructions of the Holy Spirit of God.

Imagine you are in a barbershop and the barber is doing your hair. If you do not yield your head voluntarily, what's going to happen to your hair? If one does not yield, it will obviously hinder the perfection of whatever the professional barber is trying to do. You must yield your glory (your head) to the barber or the hairdresser, whom you trust to do what he or she does best. You would not imagine they would put hazardous substances on your head, would you? Whenever the barber turns your head, you allow your head to be turned. And you know it is for your own good. Many people don't want to yield, but they want God to perfect their lives anyway. That's where we often miss it.

When you yield to God, you submit all to Him. Humble yourself in the sight of the Lord; He will lift you up. (See James 4:10.) Worship is not true worship until all is surrendered. The life of a slave is totally yielded and submitted to the master. In this case the worshiper is totally submitted and yielded to the supreme God. The will of a good servant is to fulfill the will of His master. So it is for a worshiper. The will of a true worshiper is totally yielded to the will of God, even to the point of death. A slave of Christ serves Him with every fiber of his or her being and everything he or she has, without reservation. That is total worship.

Abraham in Total Worship

Abraham was a man living in total worship. We realize that when God tested him by asking him to offer Isaac as a burnt offering, God did not want a burnt offering. Instead He wanted the heart of Abraham. Abraham passed the test. Abraham's faith is an example for all of us. He worshipped God with everything he had, without reservation. Firstly He had to leave his own people for the sake of yielding to God. Most people are not yielding, yet they are expecting to receive promises attached to yielding to God. See what the Bible says in Genesis 22:5: "And Abraham said to His young men, 'Stay here with the donkey; the lad and I will go yonder and **worship**, and we will come back to you.'"

He was willing to offer his only Son, whom he loved, in worship. If he was able to give his Son, he then could give anything to God by faith. His life and everything he had belonged to God.

A Living Sacrifice unto God

> I beseech you therefore, brethren, by the mercies of God, that you present your bodies, holy, acceptable to God, which is a reasonable service.
>
> —Romans 12:1

"Living sacrifice" refers to one who is dead to the carnal desires but alive in Christ. If one is dead to the flesh, there is no dominion of sin over him. There is a saying that "you can't kill a dead man." Being a living sacrifice is living in Christ for Christ and being dead to selfish pursuit.

The Hebrew boys—as affectionately called by many—Daniel, Meshach, Shadrach, and Abednego were good examples of lives of total worship. They refused to bow to creatures but would bow to God, the Creator. Total worship is a continuous and unconditional commitment to serving God. Daniel was put in the den of Lions. When King Nebuchadnezzar came near the den, he cried out with a lamenting voice to Daniel, "Daniel servant of the living God, **has your God, whom you serve continually**, been able to deliver you from the lions?" (Daniel 6:20). When we fully serve God, He takes it upon Himself to dispatch angels who will serve us.

Daniel was committed to humble himself every day before the Lord. He would kneel before God, seeking His face (i.e., he would engage in an act of worship), and his life was given unto God even to the point of death (i.e., he led a life of worship). He was ready to die for the sake of pleasing God. This combination is the totality of worship. Acts of worship are meaningless to God without a life of worship.

Singers versus Worshipers

One Saturday afternoon, I was coming from church and arrived at the worshippers' practice. I heard one voice I didn't personally know projecting in song with our singers. Immediately my spirit was grieved; I knew there was something wrong with him. He later asked me if he could join our church as a keyboard player, and I kindly refused. Later I discovered that he left a wife and children at their rural home and that within a week he had already proposed a couple of ladies. He had been migrating from ministry to ministry because he didn't want to repent. Then I started to understand why I was not happy with him. He had a good voice and was musically talented, but he was not a worshipper. A worshipper's daily life will reflect their unreserved reverence, love and humility toward God.

In most cases we often refer to those who lead in music as worshippers. Truly, singers are not always worshippers. Some just sing for money and don't love God. I have seen many who will play musical instruments but will then go chat on the phone when the word is being preached. Such is not a worshipper. A true and best worshipper may be a person who can't even try to sing. Yet we do not call them worshippers; this I consider an error. Those who lead in worship must be consecrated unto God. Then they can be called worshippers. You can never worship God any better than the life style you live. The offering of the wicked is an abomination.

Sacred to God

> Then Jesus said to him, "away with you, satan! For it is written, 'You shall worship the Lord your God, and **Him only you shall serve.'"**
> —Matthew 4:10

Worship is sacred, meant only for God, the Creator of the universe. This is exactly what Paul was highlighting when he said, "Therefore God also gave them up to uncleanness, in the Lust of their hearts, to dishonour their bodies among themselves, who exchanged the truth of God for the lie, and **worshipped and served the creature rather than the creator,** who is blessed forever" (Romans 1:24–25).

Worship means yielding your total life to the only highest power and authority. Only the most high God holds that place. Worship is exclusive to God. Anything else put in the place of God would only be an idol, for such a thing is not really a god. As Paul said, "... though they knew God, they did not glorify Him as God, nor were thankful, but became futile in their thoughts, and their foolish hearts were darkened. Professing to be wise they became fools, and changed the glory of the incorruptible God into an image made like corruptible man-and birds and four-footed animals and creeping things" (21–23).

Idolatry is one of the greatest sins man can ever commit. And it seems that the common idol nowadays is not graven images, but carnality. As it is written, "you shall worship no other god..." (Exodus 34:14). This is why Mordecai could not bow or pay homage to Haman. (See Ester 3:2.) The Hebrew boys in Babylonian captivity could not bow to the statue of King Nebuchadnezzar. They would rather lose their lives instead of losing communion with their Creator. (See Daniel 8–18.) Bowing to other things affects your communion with God. Whatever you bow or yield to is your god. We must be careful what we yield our lives to. Worship belongs only to the one true God. On the other hand, the Devil will never have power over those who bow only to God, the Creator of heaven and the earth.

Falling prostrate is a way of recognizing the deity of God as being the only one to be worshipped because He alone is holy in majesty, in power, and in glory. He is unparalleled, incomparable, immeasurable, and unfathomable. To fall prostrate is to yield one's total being (every atom, physically and spiritually) unto God as the Most High, in truth and in spirit. Total worship is the life of total consecration unto God. A worshipper walks in the full consciousness of holiness. Total worship cannot happen unless we are holy. Holiness is the state of being set apart for a special purpose. Holiness is conformity to the purpose of our calling. This can happen only when we discover that there is only one God and that as such only He can be worshipped.

On the other hand, idolatry is detestable to God. That was the main reason the children of Israel were often captured as slaves or oppressed by foreign nations who did not have a relationship with God. (See Judges 3:1–8.) We find that God's anger could be kindled to such a point that he would kill someone for worshipping other gods instead of the one true God, the Creator of the heavens and the earth. A good example is seen in Acts 12:21–24, where the angel struck King Herod: "So on the set day Herod arrayed in royal apparel, sat on his throne and gave an oration to them. And the people kept shouting, "the voice of a god and not a man!" Then immediately an angel of the Lord struck him, because he did not give glory to God. And he was eaten by worms and died. But the word of God grew and multiplied."

Jehovah wants us to know that beside Him there is no other God. (See Isaiah 43:10.) As such, only He is to be worshipped. He is a jealous God (Deuteronomy 6:15). He is jealous about you, and He can't share you with another.

Differences Between Praise and Worship

I grew up in an environment where the difference between praise and worship was determined by the tempo of the song. Traditionally, if the song is a bit faster, it is regarded as praise. A slower song is regarded as a song of worship. I have even heard people singing a song and saying, "My God, my God, why have you forsaken me?" during a slow part and calling it worship. What a mistake. I lived in this situation for a long time. When I discovered what true worship was, I was shocked to know how much I had actually missed out on.

Though praise and worship are almost inseparable, there is a difference. We worship God because we recognize that He is one true God and we are actively aware of His holy and glorious attributes.

However, we usually praise God because we are full of gratitude for what He has done for us in Christ.. Worship and praise can be differentiated by the contents of the words. Worship is an acknowledgment of who God is, and it is transmitted to him by actions or words. Worship is based on the revelation of the Godhead—His deity, attributes, qualities, and characters. These glorious truths are then expressed back to Him from the depths of our hearts.

Praise, on the other hand, is part of worship. Generally, praise means "to speak well of" and is often interwoven with thanksgiving. It also means "to give thanks to God," usually for what He has done. It is an appreciation of what God has done. Worship is particular to God, while praise can also be directed to man. We often praise our children when they do well at school. We often praise our workers in order to acknowledge and to motivate them. When praise is directed to God, it becomes a supernatural spiritual transaction.

CHAPTER 4

The Acts of Worship

There are words that paint a good picture of the acts used to deeply express our worship to God. Remember that true worship is the state of the heart. What we do or say in worship is the expression of the convictions of our hearts. We express our worship through acts and words that describe the state of our regard, esteem, value, and reverence toward God, based on the revelation we have received of Him. Among others, worship can be expressed in prayer, in song, with actions (nonverbal), with offerings and sacrifices, or with a combination of all. These expressions must always be congruent with the state of our hearts; otherwise, it will not be true worship..

Bowing Down

Bowing down in most cultures is a common form of worship. It is the most sought-after act of worship by kings, some religious leaders, and even the Devil himself. He wanted Jesus to bow in order to worship and serve him. He said to Jesus, "all these things I will give You if You will **fall down** and worship me" (Matthew 4:9). But Jesus replied, "For it is written, 'You shall worship the Lord your God, and Him only you shall serve'" (Matthew 4:9–10).

The act of bowing down paints a picture of total surrender and of extreme submission to God. Bowing down is a declaration of the deity of the one we bow to. As a worshipper, your whole life and being are submitted unto God. Bowing down signifies that you are aware that you are in the presence of the unequalled God. To bow down is to practically exalt God, seeing Him as the most high God.

The Hebrew word describing bowing in abject submission to God is *Shachah*, as used in Exodus 34:14. It expresses laying oneself prostrate or bowing facedown. It expresses the state of the heart's total submission and utmost reverence, depicting the total Lordship of God. One of the most excellent pictures depicting the expression of shachah is seen in the book of Exodus 34:8. When Moses saw the glory of God at Sinai, he bowed down and worshipped God. We see the story expanded by Moses later, in the book of Deuteronomy, as he was instructing the children of Israel. In retrospect he explains that he prostrated himself before the Lord for forty days and forty nights. It appears that for forty days and nights he kept prostrate because he was afraid that God would kill his brother, Aaron, and the people of Israel. (See Deuteronomy 9:25.) That was the deepest level of communion and even more; it is mind-boggling. No wonder he was shining when he came down from that mountain. He yielded himself to be infused and saturated with the glory of immortality.

Abraham also fell facedown as God was speaking with Him. At that moment, God pronounced a blessing to him. (See Genesis 17:3.) Man must surrender totally to the Creator, and not the creation.

But unlike Moses, we don't have to wait to see His glory physically in order to bow down. We proactively bow down by faith, for we look not at things that can be seen. In heaven the angels do it better because they can't stand when they see His glory. (See Revelation 4:10 and Revelation 5:14.) It seems that bowing down in prostrating oneself is the ultimate and universal expression of worship.

In some African cultures, such as Zulu and Venda, bowing down is expressed by almost rolling on the ground or floor. Whenever the king appears, they bow down, and some even roll while uttering praises and greetings of respect. In Zulu they say, for example, "Bayede or bayethe; wena wezulu." This means "Hail the king, who is as vast as the heavens [or "who is in the heavens"]." And in Venda they say "Re ya vha lotsha" while lying prostrate on the floor. "Re ya vha lotsha" means "we worship you." It means you can't be in the presence of the king and stand face-to-face with him. They lie prostrate on the floor until the king has passed or permits them to do otherwise.

To bow down is to say you can't stand in His presence. To bow down is to declare His greatness, His holiness, and His majesty. It is the reverence of His presence. The Bible says the angels in heaven bow down and take off their crowns. Even better, let me quote it from the *New Living Translation*:

… Day and night they never stop saying:

"Holy, holy, holy is the Lord God Almighty, who was and is and is to come."

Whenever the living creatures give glory , honour and thanks to Him who sits on the throne and who lives forever and ever, the twenty-four fall down before Him who sits on the throne , and worship Him who lives forever and ever. They lay their crowns before the throne and say:

"you are worthy our Lord and God, to receive glory and honour and power, for you created all things, and by your will they were created and have their being," (Revelation 4:8–11).

Kneeling Down

Another act close to bowing down is kneeling down. The Hebrew word describing this act of worship is *Barak*, which refers to kneeling in adoration. The word *adoration* holds a sense of being deeply in love. This act is often expressed in movies when one gets on his knees to propose; it should speak volumes. It is supposed to say words that the lips cannot summarize right there. It means "I am deeply and sincerely in love, and I can't help it." He who kneels down is totally surrendered under the power of love. Psalm 95:6 says, "Oh come, let us worship and bow down; Let us kneel before our maker. For He is our God, and we are the people of His pasture."

Lifting Hands

Another Hebrew word, *yadah*, refers to the lifting or throwing of the hands toward heaven in worship to God. Lifting the hands has a significant meaning in worship. It is a sign of gratitude, reverence, and perfect submission. Throwing up our hands in praise and worship is a display of internal total surrender and dependency on God. Psalm 134:2 says, "Lift up your hands in the sanctuary and bless the Lord."

Making Music

In our days, music seems to be the most common way of praise and worship. Some church circles know no other form of worship except through music. I have been to several services in which a speaker has said, "Now is time for praise and worship," followed by fast-paced or dance songs and then slow-paced songs, after which the Word was preached. It seems that for some people, praise and worship are confined to music.

Though highly effective, music is but a fraction of many forms and acts of worship. The Hebrew word for making music is *Zamae*. It refers to making music with all instruments, accompanied with voice. (See Psalm 57:7–8.) The psalmist also says, "It is good to give thanks to the Lord, and to **sing praises** to your name, o Most High; to declare your loving-kindness in the morning, and your faithfulness every night, on an instrument of ten strings, on the lute, and on the harp, with harmonious sound. For you, Lord, have made me glad through Your work; I will triumph in the works of your hands" (Psalm 92:1–4).

Clapping of Hands

The Hebrew word for clapping of hands and making a joyful noise is *Tehilah*. This clapping is intended to applaud the work of God in your life. It is meant to glorify God for His wondrous works. The shouting and clapping of praise is expressed in Psalm 47:1–4: "Oh clap your hands, all you peoples! Shout to God with the voice of triumph! For the Lord Most High is awesome; He is a great King over all the earth. He will subdue the peoples under us, and the nations under our feet. He will choose our inheritance for us, The excellence of Jacob whom He loves. Selah."

Praise with Loud Tone

Whenever God manifests Himself, we are filled with awe and joy. Then we praise God with a loud voice. In Hebrew this is referred to as to "*Shabach*." This refers to addressing and praising with a loud tone, as in Psalm 66:1, Psalm 98:4, and Psalm 95:1–2.

Praise is what we give and should give to God every day of our lives. (See Revelation 1:6.) As the Bible says, "... in everything give thanks; for this is the will of God for you in Christ Jesus for you" (1 Thessalonians 5:18).

Giving a Testimony

> They defeated him by the blood of the lamb and by the **word of their testimony.**
>
> —Revelation 12:11

A Testimony of Jesus can be a praise offering. *Halal* is the Hebrew word referring to showing off, boasting about, or celebrating God's works. It refers to God's miraculous works of redemption and salvation.

Every testimony must declare that Jesus is the Son of God, that He came in flesh and that He rose from the dead. Most so-called testimonies do not point to Jesus but are selfish boasting that points to our own abilities, as if we are blessed ourselves. A testimony pointing to Jesus is worship.

Sometimes in my life when I face challenges and feel down, when it is difficult to even come up with Scriptures to confront my situation, I start by worshipping and thanking God for what He did for me in the past. I remind Him of how I was stranded and He came through for me. When I do that, my spirit always rises, and doubt and fear get buried. Faith rises and boldly gains ascendency over every voice and imagination that exalts itself against the knowledge of God. I am then flooded with Scriptures and revelations. Victory becomes very sure.

We defeat him by the words of our testimonies. This is the reason why God wanted Moses to always record the account of how they crossed the Red Sea, how they were divinely fed in the desert and preserved—so that generations and generations could use it as a testimony. That is why Moses had to keep some manna in the covenant box—to always remind the children of Israel that God had been their provision in the wilderness. Today we have a testimony that Jesus rose from the dead and ascended to the Father. He is above death, above principalities and powers and dominions. Thus He said, "he that believes, the works which I do he will do, because I am going to the father" (John 14:13). The testimony of His resurrection gives us authority and power.

Worship by Offering and Sacrifices

> And walk in love, as Christ also has loved us and given Himself for us, an offering and **sacrifice to God for a sweet-smelling aroma.**
>
> —Ephesians 5:2

> I beseech you therefore brethren, by the mercies of God, that you present your bodies **a living sacrifice**, Holy, acceptable to God, which is your **reasonable service**.
>
> —Romans 12:1

An offering offered in faith will always be a sweet-smelling aroma unto God. I often am surprised when one brings an offering to God as if it is a common thing. Whatever you sacrifice as an offering unto God is sanctified and glorified. It brings pleasure to God. So we cannot afford to be indifferent about it. Our attitude must never be casual. Sacrifice and offering must always be done with the attitude of worship. The Scripture above shows that offering our bodies as holy and acceptable to God is a reasonable service. "Service" means "worship in the context of total surrender in ministering to God." Our offerings are used by God to test our hearts.

In Genesis 22, we read that God tested Abraham by asking him to offer his only son, whom he loved, as a burnt offering. This meant that Isaac was going to not only die but also be burnt to ashes. Remember, Isaac was the only son, the promised child. God wanted that child. When Abraham obeyed, the angel of God said, "... now I know that you fear God ..." (Genesis 22:12). It is made clear that God did not want Isaac; He wanted Abraham's heart. Everything we are asked to offer on the altar is just a test of love and fear of the Lord. Paul speaks to the people of Corinth regarding collections and says to them, "I am testing the sincerity of your love by the diligence of others" (1 Corinthians 8:6). More often the activation of our blessing is preceded by a test. So the question is, can you pass the test?

> In the Old Testament, worship would not be complete without a sacrifice. Worship was predominantly accompanied by burnt offerings on the altar. An offering is an acknowledgment of His deity. The first time offerings were burned, God did not demand them

to be offered in accordance with the law. Abel offered by revelation. On the other hand, we cannot say the same with his brother, Cain. Had Cain offered by revelation, it would have been of faith and pleasing to God. It seems that every time you bring an offering to the altar, you are actually worshipping God.

Our tithes and offerings are acts of praise and worship. There is a spiritual significance in them when they are offered in faith. In them we acknowledge God as El Shaddai. We acknowledge that He is the one who gives us power to make wealth. (See Deuteronomy 8:18–19.) Our tithes and offerings are holy unto God, for through them we honour Him. We honor the Lord with our substance. (See Proverbs 3:9.)

CHAPTER 5

Communion With God

The Grace of Our Lord Jesus Christ, and the love of God, and the communion **of the Holy Spirit** be with you all.

—2 Corinthians 13:14

Worship is a divine communion with God. There is nothing natural about it. It is more than conversation with God. It is a deep communion with God. Fellowship with God is a supernatural experience of God. Once again, of all Christian experiences, communion with God is the greatest of them. This was the ultimate reason for creation. Man was created to commune with God. Christianity is not a set of rules to follow; rather, it is a personal relationship with the Father. It is through worship that we lay bare not only before God but also in Him, and He in us through Christ. We are in His presence by faith though His Spirit. He also lays His substance to our exposure and inundates us with His very own glory. It is through deep communion that the divine elements of God flow through us.

The Holy Spirit Is the Father

I heard a preacher say, "You can't pray to the Holy Spirit." I thought to myself, *Here comes confusion.* It seems that, at some point, the more we want to simplify the understanding of the trinity of the Godhead, the more we complicate it. It seems there are not enough words to exactly describe the mystery of the divine triune God. Sometimes you get the sense that the Holy Spirit is a separate person from the Father. You almost get the idea that there are three Gods in heaven. It's an error to try explaining anything of the Holy Spirit separate from the Father and the Son. The Bible says God is that Spirit. (See 2 Corinthians 3:18.) God was in Christ, reconciling the world to Himself. If you have seen Christ, you have seen the Father. (See 2 Corinthians 5:19.) Just as it is impossible to separate man from his spirit, so is the case with God. Can you imagine someone trying to treat you in three parts, separately? It would be weird, wouldn't it? Yet your spirit is able to proceed from you and affect someone miles away from you. There are no boundaries to the human spirit. The Holy Spirit proceeds from the Father but is not a separate person. The Holy Spirit is the core of God. His voice is the voice of the Father. His feelings are the feelings of the Father. God communes with us through His Holy Spirit.

So as we fellowship with the Holy Spirit, we are fellowshipping with the Godhead: Father, Son, and Holy Spirit. Worship is one of the great mysteries of the kingdom.

Communion of the Lord's Supper

I used to wonder what it meant to say the Lord's Supper is a communion. Jesus sat with the disciples around one table. They shared of the same bread (His flesh) and of the fruit of the vine (His blood). As sure as the disciples were aware of the presence of Jesus at that table, so should we be, by faith. As they heard His voice, so should we. We must share with Him in everything. During Communion, the love is practically spread across all worshippers. The power of the blood is practically manifested across all the souls partaking.

Practical Fellowship

> And He gave unto Moses, when He had made an end **of communing with him** upon Mount Sinai, two tables of testimony, tables of stone written with the finger of God.
>
> —Exodus 31:18 KJV

The life of communion is easily seen in the relationship Moses had with God. God spoke to Him face-to-face, as a man speaks to His friend. (See Exodus 33:11.) God said about His communion with Moses, "I speak with Him face-to-face, even plainly, and not in dark sayings; and he sees the form of the Lord" (Numbers 12:8).

We discover in the book of Deuteronomy, chapter 9, verses 18–19, that Moses was not standing face-to-face with God. Instead he laid prostrate for forty days and nights. God listened to Moses' plea to spare Aaron. The atmosphere was full of reverence and awe. Through this communion, Moses was glorified. The Bible also shows in Exodus 34:35 that whenever the children of Israel saw the face of Moses, the skin of Moses' face shone; they were afraid and terrified such that Moses had to put the veil on his face again until he went back in to speak with Him.

Moses committed himself to nothing else but being with God. He knew the figure of God and the voice of God. They shared the same vision. They shared their emotions; what made God angry also made Moses angry. Moses broke the first tablets of the law, as he was angry at what the Israelites did. (See Exodus 32:19.) This is oneness in the spirit realm.

This is seen much more clearly in the life of Jesus. In John 10:30, He said, "I and the father are one." When He was praying for Lazarus, He said, "father, I thank you that you have heard me. And I know that you always hear me, but because of these people who are standing by I said this, that they may believe that you sent Me" (John 11:41–42). The Life of Jesus signified a perfect communion with God. Whenever Jesus encountered problems, He would not be startled but would rather be calm and provide a solution. He wouldn't start praying and fasting in reaction to problems. He was always ready, by continuous fellowship with God. In times of trouble He was never in shock, because He saw situations as God saw them. He simply became the solution. In this Scripture we get the sense that Jesus always spoke with God and God would always pay attention to what he said and do likewise. Were it not for the people around Him, He would not have prayed as he did, but instead, He would only have to command Lazarus to come forth.

Meaning of Communion

Before we see the experience of Moses, let's revisit what Communion means. The word *communion* is synonymous with *fellowship*. It comes from a Greek word, *Koinonia*. Fellowship is a reciprocal and active joint participation between God and a Christian. Fellowship is a union with God. The Bible says, "For we are members of His body, of His flesh and of His bones" (Ephesians 5:30). There is oneness of God and the worshipper. We cleave with God in the union of the power of the Spirit of God. It is this oneness that infuses the substance of God in a worshipper's life. Hence worshippers of Jehovah have the substance of God in glory and power.

Fellowship of the Saints

Let me give you an example of a special thing that happened in our congregation. One Easter weekend, the members decided that they were going to cook the best of the food they had in their own homes. Each person brought whatever he or she had prepared to one table so that all could eat. Some cooked the best and most expensive; others, just the usual. Yet at the point when the packages were laid on the table, there was no private ownership; rather, there was now a collective ownership. All could eat whatever they chose to eat without any wrongdoing. They gladly ate, prayed for one another, and celebrated. Those who did not have much food at home had more than enough here. As they sat together, they partook together of all that was on the table. Most did not even touch what they had brought to eat. Rather, they enjoyed what others had prepared. Those who did not have financial muscles were now strengthened by those who had more.

Such is the case in fellowship with the Holy Spirit. Through the Holy Spirit, God brings to the table His righteousness, holiness, power, wisdom, glory, and, of course, His holy blood. We then bring our sins, weaknesses, unrighteousness, and so on. He takes away that which we brought to the cross, and we take on what God brought to the table. We partake of the divine nature of God. Since we are engrafted on Him, His blood, His righteousness, His dynamic power, and His goodness are abundantly flowing through our faculties.

There is a special kind of glory and anointing brought about during worship. Fellowship for us is a time to participate in the divine nature of God. We participate in all the fullness of the redemptive benefits. We participate in our heritage.

In addition, it is not a one-way process. It is an intimate experience based on a relationship. Did you ever wonder how this happened? Let's look at the communion Moses had with God.

We Enter The Holy of Holies

> Therefore brethren, **having boldness to enter the holiest** by the blood of Jesus, by a new and living way which He consecrated for us, through the veil, that is, **His flesh**, and having a high priest over the house of God, let us draw near with a true heart in full assurance of faith, having our hearts sprinkled from an evil conscience and our bodies washed with water. Let us hold fast the confession our hope without wavering, for He who promised is faithful.
>
> —Hebrews 10:19–23

It is impossible to enter the holiest of all and not experience the presence of God. Communion with God was highly fundamental for the nation of Israel. It was during Moses' communion with God that the children of Israel received directions and instructions from God. It was during this communion that God shared His emotions, desires, and plans with Moses, such as His anger toward the Israelites. It was through the same communion that Moses interceded for the people so that God relented in His anger against the people and did not annihilate them from the face of the earth. Moses personally knew God; He knew what pleased and displeased Him. He knew exactly how to pray to God for results. Moses was empowered through a setting of deep fellowship with God; though he had weaknesses, he led the multitude of people out of Egypt. He received divine wisdom from this setting to face any challenge with audacity.

Moses' situation was very awesome and intriguing. The Bible shows that he got into the tabernacle; God descended in a cloudy pillar and covered the tabernacle. The very same pillar would block the entrance of that tabernacle while God was speaking to Moses face-to-face.

In the sanctuary, the high priest was to enter the holiest place to minister unto (worship) God. God was in there, such that if the high priest was defiled, he would not come back alive. You can't minister to someone who is not present with you. The actual presence of God was right there in the tabernacle. The Bible shows that the system of the old covenant was the shadow of real things. Yet when we imagine the glory that Moses experienced, it is awesome. Now we do not enter a place built by human hands; we enter into the holiest place by the blood of Jesus Christ. The veil was torn for us to enter by faith and worship in His presence. Hebrews 10:19–20 says, "Therefore brethren, having boldness to enter the holiest by the new and living way which He consecrated for us, through the veil, that is , His flesh." We jointly participate in the fire and share emotions and affections. When we get in there, He infuses His fire into our being; we receive His wisdom and revelations. His divine nature is imparted upon us. Christians are supposed to experience God in a much better way than Moses did. God is not a respecter of persons. Our system of worship is based on real things, not the shadow.

Worship Is Personal Communion

Worship is a direct communion and personal relationship with God. There is no middle man. You can't worship on behalf of another or vice versa. In worship, you personally come face-to-face with the Godhead and declare your heart's impression of who He is, both verbally and nonverbally. Though you could be in a crowd or in a corporate prayer, when it comes to worship the atmosphere turns into a personal sacred space. You must personally connect your heart to God's Spirit. Worship is primarily a special personal space of intimacy with God. Hence it is virtually impossible to worship God if you have no revelation of Him. You do not worship God in a third person. Can you imagine if one were to stand up and say, "Oh God, angels are worshipping you." Well, that is not necessarily wrong, but it is the same as saying, "Oh God, my brother is worshipping you; my mother says you are holy."

Imagine you have a wife and each time you intend to give her a compliment you say, "My friend says you are beautiful." What do you think her response would be? She would probably say to you, "Well, what about you? What do you say?" It's not worship on your side if you have turned yourself into a worship broker. Who gets credit for those words? I can imagine God thinking, *What about you?* In Matthew 16:13–15, Jesus Christ asked His disciples, "'… Who do men say I, the son of man am?' So they said, 'Some say John the Baptist, some Elijah, and others Jeremiah or one of the prophets.' He said to them 'But **who do you say that I am?**'"

God is deeply interested in what you say, not what you think others say about Him. So it does not matter what others say, but who you say God is. That's what matters the most—what the worshipper says about who the Godhead is, not what others say He is.

Revelation of God[3]

The efficacy of our worship is contingent upon the level of revelation of our God. I struggled for a long time with lacking revelation of God. But when I had that revelation, my faith was developed, and it helped me to connect the throne of God. I started worshipping and praising God in faith because of that revelation. The revelation of God permits us to understand the will and responsibility of our God toward us. By revelation we are able to actualize the promises of God in our lives.

One of the greatest struggles of the body of Christ is hearing His voice. Some don't expect Him to speak back. This is quite indicative of the apparent poor level of revelation of God among people in some circles. One of the hindrances to worshipping God is the lack of understanding or revelation regarding who He is. It is a grievous mistake to lack in the knowledge of God. In Isaiah 43:10, He says, "you are my servant whom I have chosen, **that you may know and believe Me and understand that I am He.**"

One mistake people make is pursuing God through secular approaches or methods of the world. It can never be enough to try knowing God through intellectual means. It is called walking in the flesh. Paul says, "Consequently, from now on we estimate and regard no one from a [purely] human point of view [in terms of natural standards of value]. [No] even though **we once did estimate Christ from a human viewpoint** and as a man, yet now [we have such knowledge of Him that] we know Him no longer [in terms of the flesh]" (2 Corinthians 5:16 AB).

---

[3]   Refer to "Knowing your God" in chapter 9.

In the *New King James Version*, the same Scripture says, "Therefore, from now on we regard no one **according to flesh**." Paul shows that He once saw Christ from the human point of view rather than through revelation.

It took being knocked down on his way to Damascus for Paul to start knowing Jesus differently. Before then, he had always thought of Jesus as a natural man, the son of Joseph the carpenter and so on. Beyond that it was blasphemous to him to suggest that Jesus was the Christ. As for the disciples, to him they were weak and deceived folks that he could slaughter without guilt. He operated as a Pharisee, meaning he was educated and felt that he somehow could speak with some authority. The turn of events came to pass when he had a revelation of our Lord, Jesus. A new relationship then ensued. He had a continuous communion with the Christ in the Holy Spirit. This accounts for the many books he wrote as letters. He was taught not by man but by the Holy Spirit of God. Deep communion brings forth more revelation. That was the case with Paul. Jesus also said to Peter, "Blessed are you, Simon Bar-Jonah, for flesh and blood has not revealed this to you, but my Father who is in heaven" (Matthew 16:17).

There is knowledge far superior to science, far above philosophy or any knowledge of the world. That is knowledge of God arrived at by revelation. We are partakers of superior wisdom, by which the heavens were stretched. The same knowledge imparts life eternal to those who believe in this good news. Though it is foolishness to the world, to us who believe, it is wisdom and power of God at work in us, even unto salvation.

You see, revelation comes not from universities but from the Father. Based on this revelation, Jesus said to Peter, "you are blessed Simon, son of Jonah, for flesh and blood has not revealed this to you, but my father who is in heaven."(See Matthews 16:17.) Kingdom principles work for those who have a revelation of the Christ of God. Later He declared that Peter was the rock and that He would build the church on the rock. The church was built on the revelation of Jesus and His relationship with the Father.

It is only when we have a hold on spiritual revelation of the Godhead that we can say we know God. Consequently, we can worship Him in spirit and in truth.

Worship Is an Affection

The sincerity of our love toward God determines our devotion to Him. Those who worship God recognize that God so loved them, even when they were sinners, that He could not withhold His only dear son. Because of Love, God gave His only begotten son, even unto death. (See John 3:16.) As a result, we received a command to love the Lord our God with all our hearts and might. (See Luke 10:27.) Worship is fellowship of Love between man and God.

The affection is that of a father-and-son relationship, which comes through righteousness, by faith. A worshipper therefore lives a life of deep adoration. The effect of love in our Christian lives can never be overstated. The love of God compels us to enter into a place of deep fellowship. Our Christian covenant is based on the motivation of love. Remember the most famous Scripture "For God so loved the world and gave His only begotten son …" (John 3:16). True worship can never be devoid of love. Love is the greatest and main ingredient of our life of worship.

First Love or Nothing

In our relationship with Him, God requires nothing less than first love. It's either first love or nothing. We are deeply in love with God. It was the case with the church of Ephesus. He says to her (the church in Ephesus) in the book of Revelation 2:4–5, "Nevertheless I have this against you, **that you have left the first love.** Remember where you have fallen and repent and do the first works, or else I will come to you and quickly and remove your lampstand from its place."

In the above Scripture, we see God commending the church of Ephesus for their patience, hard works for His name, how they tested those who claimed to be the apostles, and how they persevered. But He turned around and said, "Nevertheless I have this against you." This cancels out the good report. Their good work is reduced to nothing if this one thing is not fulfilled. Because of it God promises to remove the lampstands from the midst of the church if they do not repent. The lampstands represent the real church. If the lampstand is removed, the church remains a mere congregation. The congregation cannot remain a church if the lampstand is removed. Many may still congregate, but the church is no more because the lampstands have been removed as a result of the absence of first love. Therefore, the acts of worship mean very little to God if they are void of first love from the heart.

Worship is an expression of reverence unto God. As it is written, "Therefore since we are receiving a kingdom which cannot be shaken, let us have grace, by which **we may serve God acceptably with reverence and godly fear**" (Hebrews 12:28).

Worship is affection. We can't say we worship God and yet be emotionally and spiritually indifferent. We must worship with all our passion, our love, and our full reverence unto God. Without love we are like an empty drum. Love is the greatest. (See 1 Corinthians 13:13.)

CHAPTER 6

Upside Down: Inverted Order of Priorities

Therefore do not worry, saying, "what shall we eat?' or 'what shall we drink?' or 'what shall we wear?' for after these things the gentiles seek. For your father knows what that you need all these things. But seek first the kingdom of God and His righteousness and all these things shall be added to you.

—Matthew 6:31–33

When our number-one priority is to pursue God, we have authority over the natural realm, the materials, and the supplies for this life. Jesus commands us to seek first the kingdom of God and its righteousness; then the materials will be added to us. Yet we are often tempted to do the opposite. We live in a materialistic and scientific generation. It seems more natural to put value on things that we can touch, see, hear, smell, and so on. Atheism is based on this line of reasoning. From a young age we invest money, time, and resources to educate our kids to reason based on empirical evidence and systematic and logical methods. We learn to completely and wholly trust and depend on natural laws. This we must do, but not at the expense of knowing God. When we focus on one side of a phenomenon at the expense of another of equal or higher importance, it is a costly error.

We must seek to do the will of God first. In this generation, we try our best to make our lives better based on temporary things, and yet the real life is in the spirit realm—Christ. Christianity is the life beyond the limited flesh. We look not on things that can be seen, but on things that can't be seen. A believer must understand that the natural world is limited and will pass away. The spiritual world is more durable and conceives the natural one.

People can do anything to get material wealth. They can sell their souls to gain everything material. With the advent of prosperity preaching, we also changed our soul-winning or evangelistic strategies. I often hear people inviting others to church with the promise of material increase. As a result, we lose the essence and the order of priorities. Though prosperity is the real part of our salvation, we shouldn't point people to prosperity instead of Jesus. Oftentimes when such people come, because they are not being pointed at Christ, they miss the point. When they think things are not happening as they wanted, they start complaining and leave the church. Materialistic people can sell God. That's why people join cults that will require them to kill family and friends to promote wealth. This is idolatry at its worst. God says, "Do not have anything that will take the place of God" (IJohn 5:21 NLT).

The same mentality is often operating in the church. For some church folks joy and happiness depends on materialism. Worship is often based on sensual reasoning. They actually have little or no consciousness of personal fellowship with God. Some of them pray or come to church only when they have problems; others pray for them, and then they disappear.

Instead of being materialistic, we worship God because we know He is God, by faith. Our worship is completely unconditional. We fellowship with Him no matter what we face. I still admire the generation that cherished martyrdom. They knew the value of living and dying for

Christ. I was awestruck by someone who said, "God, thank you for the opportunity to suffer for you." We need to realize that wealth and prosperity are by-products of our fellowship with God, and not visa versa. Some people fellowship with God for what He can give. We must be like our Lord Jesus; in pursuing the will of God, He said His food was to do the will of Him who sent Him. (See John 4:34.)

Compelling Hunger for God

Blessed are they that hunger and thirst for righteousness.
—Matthew 5:6

The greatest of blessings comes when we are hungrier for God than we are for what He can give to us. Whatever you receive from God is a manifestation of His presence in you. When you hunger to be filled with the Spirit of God, you get filled with power, for it is written, "but you shall receive power when the Holy Spirit come upon you" (Acts 1:8). This means that our hunger must be a hunger to be filled with the Spirit and to fellowship with Him. The power will follow, tongues will follow, and prophecies will follow. Most people just want the power, the prophecies, and the tongues instead of Him who is the source and carrier of all these. Great is the man who is fully aware that his need for God is greater than all the wealth of the world. When these truths dawn in your spirit, you will not exchange them for anything in the whole wide world. We become better worshippers when we discover that He is everything to us. Our hunger and thirst are forces that drive our desire to see God. When we have this kind of hunger, we will chase not miracles but the God of miracles. We will not chase power but hunger for the God of power.

Praise and Worship Are the Answer

For most people, the first logical step when in trouble is petition. I discovered that the most powerful and effective form of prayer is worship.

The most incredible incident where the power of worship was quite apparent is recorded in Acts 16. Paul and Silas were severely punished and locked up in an inner cell. After being chained and guarded, they, by faith, started to praise and worship the most high God.

Praise is giving thanks and commending the goodness or ability of God. But let us be honest, naturally the situation they were in did not warrant any form of praise or thanksgiving. These guys, however, did not focus on the pains, their shackles, or the prison. They did not complain to God for allowing them to be punished; nor did they blame Him for not getting them out of prison. But guess what happened—He got them out anyway. Not only did they get out, but they also got out in style. The jailer took them home and nursed them. The tables were turned because of worship. Victory is guaranteed to a worshipper. Live a life of worship, and you will live a life of victory. The one who bows before God can stand before any situation. When we chase God, we have authority over the material. When we pursue the material, the material becomes our God. A carnal mind is enmity against God, and they that are in the flesh cannot please God. (See Romans 8:7–8.)

Full of Thanks and Gratitude[4]

Worship cannot be without thanksgiving unto God. We look at what Jesus went through in our stead, and we are thankful. Colossians 2:6–7 says, "as you therefore have received Christ Jesus the Lord, so walk in him, rooted and built up in Him and established in the faith, as you have been taught, **abounding in it with thanks giving.**"

---

[4]   Refer to soaking prayers: chapter 8, point 4.

CHAPTER 7

Power of Worship

When we bow down to worship God in the face of inevitable destruction, the almighty God stands up to fight our battles. Praise and worship will always bring the best out of God. Even in the natural realm, whenever we praise people around us, they tend to bring out the best they have. Praise and worship are guaranteed to always bring forth significant results in our lives. They will always arouse an aura of power and glory, the atmosphere that will always change your situations. When all else has failed, when we have tried everything and have done all we know how, to no avail, we look to God and worship the Lord our God. God feels deep pleasure and satisfaction in praise and worship. When we trust in God, we cannot be disappointed. True worship Glorifies and honors God, yet it doesn't change Him even a bit. Instead worship releases the power and the glory of God, to the benefit of the worshipper.

The body of Christ is never meant for defeat. No Christian should be defeated. In everything, we are made to be more than conquerors through Him who loved us. (See Romans 8:37.) The weapons of our warfare are not carnal, but mighty through God to the pulling down of strongholds. (See 2 Corinthians 10:3.) A believer holds a place of supremacy over the world by worshipping God. We hail from higher grounds. Those who live in total worship often experience an abundance of grace that an average believer is unfamiliar with. God requires that we worship Him, yet our worship is of more benefit to us than it is to God. God has a soft spot for worship, and His favor will always be inclined toward the worshipper. People who have been used by God lived their lives in worship.

Tables Are Turned

Our troubles will always present us with the best opportunities to see the greatness of God. When we face challenges that are beyond our capacity to handle, we know it a critical time to worship. Worship will turn the tables against your enemies. It will make you to gain ascendency over your enemies. Remember the walls of Jericho; they came crashing down because of worship. Remember Paul and Silas; while feeling the pain, having been shackled in chains and guarded in the inner cell, they praised and worshipped God. Naturally speaking, there was no way out for them. From a human standpoint, they would be justified in complaining to God. They were wrongly suffering at the hands of the oppressor, yet we say God is able? It would have been justifiable to question the authenticity of the Word. But Jesus said, "lo, I am with you always, even to the end of the age" (Matthew 28:20). On the contrary, they worshipped even when there was no sign of a way out. This shows us that their lives where consecrated to God even unto death.

While they were singing and praising God, they heard an earthquake. All the stocks were broken loose and all the doors flew open—not some of the doors, but all doors, because the heavens can't resist worship. Their jailer wanted to kill himself, but at last he took them from prison to his own home to nurse their wounds and entertain them. Even more importantly, God was glorified when the jailer and his family accepted Jesus Christ. The tables were turned; the person who was supposed to be keeping them in jail was now taking instructions from his own prisoners. May the tables be turned in your favor, in Jesus' name. When we bow down to worship God in the face of inevitable destruction, the almighty God stands up to fight our battles.

Jonah, while in the belly of the big fish in the midst of the ocean, did not complain. He worshipped and praised God. The fish was propelled to the shore because Jonah acknowledged God. May your fish vomit you upon the shore of your billowing oceans. As you worship God, may your troubles usher you into your destiny.

Platform for Hearing God

Most people miss their seasons because they can't hear God. Many times I have heard people say, "I have prayed, and God has not answered my prayer." God always answers prayer of faith. True worship creates a platform to experience the manifested presence of God. I have experienced this personally. The Bible is full of such examples. When you worship in spirit and in truth, your spiritual antennae are tuned to hear and see God. You become more aware of God's presence, and the spiritual realm is more tangible. Oh that we may live a life of total worship. Somebody said, "Do not pray that God will speak to you; rather pray that you may hear God" (author unknown). Most people can't recognize God's voice, and they then blame God for not answering their prayers.

When I was facing academic challenges, I started to worship, and lightning flashed from haven. It was while worshipping the following day that I heard a voice saying, "The lightning you saw is a Scripture." I was very sure it was God speaking to me. That made me to continue worshipping God even more than before. Then my situation changed.

In the Bible we find that, on some occasions, God chose to manifest Himself through the angels. A good example is when the angel Gabriel came to announce the birth of John the Baptist. At that time Zachariah was busy serving (ministering to) God according to the custom of the priest's office. The angel announced that His prayer has been heard and therefore Elisabeth would bear him a son to be called John. When the priest showed some doubt, the angel said "I am Gabriel that stand in the presence of God; and am sent to speak unto you these good news." (See Luke 1:8–19.) God was present, for the angel that was speaking to Zechariah was standing in the presence of God. Yet God chose to present Himself (His word) through the angel.

In another instance we see, in the book of Acts 13:2–3, that "As they ministered to the Lord and fasted, the Holy Spirit said, now separate for me Barnabas and Saul for the work to which I have called them." Then having fasted and prayed and laid hands on them, they sent them away."

Healed from Piles

Just recently, I was worshipping and praising God when God showed me that there was someone who would be healed from piles during the following Sunday service. On that Sunday, while I was conducting a prayer of declaration, I said by faith that someone was going to be healed from piles. One week went past, and then on the second week, a lady came to me and said, "Pastor! You remember when you said someone with piles would be getting healed?" With great interest, I said yes. She said, "It was me. My rectum was coming out, and I was billed for an operation the following week. But when you announced that someone was getting healed, the rectum went back inside. I am now completely healed, and the operation has been cancelled."

Two months later another brother came and said "Pastor, I also had piles, and when you said someone would be getting healed from piles, I received my healing."

The Boldness of Faith

True worshippers have the boldness of faith. This is boldness not from self-confidence, but from Jesus confidence. They look beyond their own weaknesses and trust in the power from heaven. They know there is treasure in their earthen vessels against which no human obstacle or demonic cohort can stand. We understand that Daniel served (ministered to) God continuously. Remember, "to minister" means "to worship." This means Daniel was forever in the presence of God consciously. Those who minister to God are always conscious of His presence with them.

One day, my two-year-old boy was playing outside the house and the gate was not properly closed. I was surprised to see him running, rushing in with a terrified look. When I looked outside, I saw he was running away from the dog from next door. When I went outside to chase off the dog, I was amazed at what the boy did. He went ahead of me, commanding the dog to get off the yard, with great boldness. I started thinking to myself, *This is how Christians must be. The boy has such confidence in his father that he has the audacity to chase the dog that just terrified him.* Christians can face big problems because they know God is with them. He is with us even unto the end of the age.

Christians see in the spiritual realm and know that He that is in them is greater than he that is against them. When thrown in the den of lions, Daniel was aware of the angel that shut the mouths of the lions. And years later, the author of the book of Hebrews recounted the incident: "by faith they shut the mouth of lions."

What allows such ordinary people to partake in such extraordinary things? True worship is a product of faith. By faith we recognize the presence of the invisible God and become bold—not of ourselves, but of He that is with and in us. We are more aware of the aura of the immortality around us and in us, such that a supernatural audacity is aroused in us. As a result, mortality becomes paralyzed and swallowed up. Fear and doubt fall smitten, because we are more confident of the Lord our God than we are of the predicament at hand. Daniel might have looked at the lions and yet continued His fellowship with the Father, the Lord of the armies of Israel. Moses developed the same audacity to face the most stubborn and dangerous Pharaoh, who had the power to kill.

Increasing the Level of Glory

The degree of our yielding to God will determine the degree of glory manifesting upon and among us. The glory of God, generally speaking, is the manifested presence of God. A gloried person manifests in the life and nature of God. The longer one stays in the acts worship, the more glorified one becomes. Worship is like incubation; it produces an atmosphere of glory and supernatural experiences. In worship we are in the Holy of Holies, engulfed by the incubating presence of God.

In Exodus 34 we find that Moses humbled himself in the presence of God for forty days and nights. He bowed prostrate for that long and came out shining, and he did not know it. That was in the Old Testament. We now have a more incredible situation—the tabernacle of God is with man. Look at 2 Corinthians 3:7–9:

> But if the ministry of death, written and engraved on stones was glorious, so that the children of Israel could not look steadily at the face of Moses because of the glory of the countenance , which glory was passing away, how will the ministry of the spirit not be more glorious? For if the ministry of righteousness exceeds much more in glory. For even what was made glorious had no glory in this respect, because of the glory that that excels. For if what was passing away was glorious, what remains was much more glorious.

When one is totally humbled in worship, there is an infusion and stirring up of the substance of the most high God—eternal life. The voltage of God practically runs through our blood and even the clothes we put on. I have read an amazing story of a man by the name of Pastor Richard Ngidi, as narrated by Dr. A Khathide[5].

> He used to go out into an open field to pray. As he was kneeling down praying and dedicating his life to the Lord, a poisonous snake found its way to the place where he was. Richard felt his body cringing because

---

[5] Extracted from *What a Giant of Faith* by Dr. Agrippa Khathide (Gospel Publishers, Johannesburg, 1993), 19.

he could hear the movement and the hissing of the snake, but, he did not open his eyes. He continued to call upon the name of the Lord.

Suddenly he felt something hitting his clean shaven head and when he opened his eyes, he found a big snake writhing on the ground. Ngidi touched his head where he felt the blow and he was amazed that there was no blood coming out and no wound at all. The greater surprise was when he saw the snake dying in front of his eyes without him having done anything to it.

He had bowed in the bush to pray when he heard the hissing sound of a snake coming toward him. Because he was intensely in communion, he could not give it any attention. While he was praying, the snake reached for his head for to bite it. When he opened up his eyes and looked, the snake was writhing at his feet, completely dead. What killed the snake? What prevented this man's death? The substance of God infused in his body. The glory of God is our rear guard. (See Isaiah 54:8.) The man was highly glorified. Talk of the Khabod glory. I also heard of the revival of the shining ones on our continent some time back. People would go to a restaurant not knowing their heads were shining. What was the secret? The life of surrender accounted for such experience. Yes, believers can handle snakes with safety; though they drink any deadly poison, it shall not harm them.

Platform for Miracles

Have you ever wondered how it happened that handkerchiefs and aprons were brought to touch the body of Paul and when put upon the sick, the sick were healed and demons left? I was even more astonished and intrigued when I read for the first time that Peter's shadow carried the voltage of the glory of God, such that when it touched the sick there was a transfer of virtue to heal and deliver. (See Acts 5:15.) These were constantly ministering unto God. Worship and praise create a supernatural atmosphere for miracles. The apostles' lives were poured as sacrifices unto God. Their acts of worship were intensely genuine.

The atmosphere of worship releases the overflow of anointing that breaks yokes. Most of the times during worship we experience divine interventions. We have read the story of Paul and Silas in Acts 16, in which tables where turned because they focused not on the situation but on God. We have seen the crippled and lame walking during praise and worship. Stupendous miracles do happen during praise and worship. Demons often manifest and leave people during praise and worship.

Soaking Prayers

Effective prayers are always soaked in praise and worship. Intermingling supplications with praise and worship releases the potency of faith. And nothing shall be impossible to him that believes. I have looked at prayers that produced tremendous results; they were preceded by and intermingled with praises and worship. As Paul said, "be anxious for nothing, but in everything by prayer and supplication, **with thanksgiving**, let your requests be made known to God" (Philippians 4:6). This means prayer requests must go to God with thanksgiving (praises). We have seen this in the book of Acts. When the Christians were persecuted for preaching the gospel, they then sought the face of God and said, "**Lord, You are God**, who made the heaven and earth and the sea and all that is in them" (Acts 4:24). They didn't start by asking God to do one, two, or three things. Instead they started by declaring that He is God (that is worship) and stating what He did (He is the Creator). That's how prayer of faith should be. The Bible says they that come to Him must believe that He is and that He is the one who rewards those who seek Him diligently. (See Hebrews 11:6.)

Whenever you declare God in the face of and contrary to your problem, the problem is bound to bow before you. Jehoshaphat approached God the same way. When he discovered that the army of the enemies was great, he feared. However, most importantly he sought the Lord, God of the armies of Israel. He said, "Oh Lord God of our fathers, are you not God in the Heaven, and do you not rule over all the kingdoms of the nations, and in your hand is there not power and might so that no one is able to withstand you?" (2 Chronicles 20:6).

He approached God with great confidence and trust. We worship in the face of problems because we know our God; He is greater than all.

CHAPTER 8

Unconditional Worship

In every thing give thanks; for this is the will of God
in Christ Jesus for you.

—I Thessalonians 5:18

Whether we are in the valley or going up the mountain, we must worship God. Worship is unconditional. It does not matter how we feel, or what we see with our eyes. It does not matter what we have or do not have. Nothing we go through can ever change His love, His glory and power. Even in the face of death, He is God. In everything, give thanks to God.

A Simple, Encouraging Story

One time while at the university, I heard the story of a young man who did not have proper shoes but only a pair of worn-out sandals. Apparently someone had promised to give him shoes, but unfortunately the promise was not fulfilled. The young man was bothered by this such that it would disturb him when it was time to worship. One day while worshipping, he was focusing on not having shoes, wondering why God was not giving him shoes. Instead of worshipping, he was blaming God. But as the worship progressed, he just looked up and said, "Shoes or no shoes, praise the Lord." The young man had finally come to the revelation of true worship. Worshipping God depends only on one condition—that the Lord Jehovah is God. Everything else hinges on this truth.

When we worship, it means that we have more confidence in our God than in our apparent situations. Most Christians worship God when every thing seems to be going well. I hear people saying, "We thank God because we are not sick and we are still alive." What will they do the day they are attacked by sickness or face death? Will they still worship God? If we worship God based on such things, that is carnality. It is walking in the flesh. Yet the Bible says we walk by faith and not by sight. (See 2 Corinthians 5:7.) It is also written that we look not at the things that can be seen, but at the things that cannot be seen. (See 2 Corinthians 4:18.) Neither death nor life shall take us away from the love of God.

Paul and Silas worshipped God in the midst of pain. They received severe punishment for serving God when they cast out a demon from the damsel. Then they were apprehended and put under a jailor's charge. The jailer then thrust them into the inner cell and fastened them with stocks. They did not start saying, "Why us, Lord?" They never said, "Why did you allow this to happen to us Lord?" Instead they started singing and praising God. (See Acts 16:23–40.) Their predicament could not in any way dampen their trust in God. I am trying to think of what song they may have sung. Maybe they sang "You Are Faithful, Oh Lord," or even "He Never Failed Me Yet." They stirred up the heavens, angels rushed down and shook the foundations of the prison, and shackles flew open. Oh, praise God, for those who know their God shall be strong and do exploits.

People who know God are not fazed by what they see or observe in the flesh. They see beyond situations. How many people can look in an empty fridge and thank God for providing them with what is more than sufficient? How many people can thank God for healing while feeling pain in their bodies? Those who do so will see what they thank God for.

One day I was coming back from buying stock from a direct marketing company called Angel Your Life. I started to feel a pain in my hip. It was as though it were dislocated; the pain was unbearable. I started confessing that I had been healed by His stripes and rebuked the pain. The pain persisted until I arrived home and parked the car. I decided to collect my son on foot from his day care center because I wanted to exercise my faith. I walked through the gate limping, and I started praising God for healing me. I said, "Thank you, Father, for healing me. By His stripes I was healed; I remain healed and will always be healed. Thank you, Jesus, for taking away my infirmities and my diseases. It's not possible for me to be sick now. Thank God I am healed. Thank you, God; I am healed." I said that many times until it sank into my heart. When I arrived at the day care center I had forgotten that I had experienced pain.

Praise and worship must never be dependent on how we feel or on our situations. Instead, when we worship in the face of situations, our troubles will be changed. We often say "Thank you, Lord" even when we don't feel thankful. We confess the goodness of God in the midst of pain. We thank God for keeping our children safe even when the Devil whispers the opposite. Even when we feel like crying, we say "Thank you, Lord." You are faithful, oh God; every day and every hour, you are faithful.

It does not matter what we are going through; God is able, faithful, and remains God. The problem is, we are often oblivious of what God is doing. It happened to the servant of Elisha. He saw the Enemy and he became terrified. Yet the armies of the Lord of Hosts were already dispatched to protect the man of God, but he could not see them. The man of God instead was in great peace because he saw and focused on the armies of God. Then he prayed that God would open the eyes of his servant, and he saw the armies of God—horses and chariots of fire round about Elisha (See 2 Kings 6:15–20.) That is the reason the just shall live by faith and not by sight.

As Daniel prayed, God answered immediately, but it took twenty-one days before the answer manifested to Daniel. He could have given up, thinking that God had not answered. The Devil might have preached to him, "You have prayed for twenty days now; God will never answer." God always answers prayers, but are you at the right place to receive?

The Reality of the Spiritual Things

It is often easy for someone to start worshipping when he or she sees a miracle. It is easy to be stirred up into praise and worship when you see what God has already done. If we are to wait for a miracle before we start worshipping, then we will miss many miracles. If we maintain such a mindset, it is therefore no longer faith. The essence of faith is to be able to see the concreteness of the spiritual things and depend on them and act on them as though they have been physically manifested. By faith we have the evidence of things that naturally can't be seen. Worship is carried out by faith, for we reckon that what we hope for is now a substance. The Bible says that when you believe this, you shall have whatever you say.

New Kidneys from Heaven

A miracle is not making something out of nothing. Rather it is converting the spiritual realities into material realities. One day we were praying for a lady who had kidney problems; her doctor had recommended a kidney transplant. I told her that God has a storeroom full of new parts, including kidneys. We started thanking God for giving her new kidneys as we also rebuked sickness. She went for a checkup, and her doctor asked her what medication she had been using. He was surprised at what had happed. He gave her a clean bill of health after about two to three months of hospitalization.

We were thanking God for her new kidneys because there was a reality of new kidneys in the Spirit. However, her body could not use them in that nature, so they had to be converted. A miracle is the retrieval from the spirit realm of whatever you need to use in the physical realm. When we worship, we are more conscious of the spiritual things.

To us, things that can't be seen are a substance. We possess them. Life begins in the spirit realm.

The Cost of Complaining

> Then they despised the pleasant land; they did not believe His word, **but they complained in their tents** , and did not heed the voice of the Lord. Therefore He raised His hand in an oath against them, to overthrow them in the wilderness.
>
> —Psalm 106:24–26

Praise and worship in times of trouble have proven to be the most effective ways to change the circumstances in my life. Unfortunately, just as praise and worship are so powerful, so is complaining. Every time we complain, we release the negative energies, which work against us. I discovered that all along, as I was complaining, I was working against myself. I did not see what I was losing, because I was thinking it was God's fault. And that's where the Enemy desires to quarantine you. We understand from the Bible that the children of Israel quarantined themselves in a desert for forty years by complaining to God. The journey that could have taken just few days turned into circles around the dry and barren place because of their unbelief. Quarreling is a result of unbelief. Every time we quarrel because of unbelief, we are considered rebellious. When we do this, we should never think that we will receive anything from God.

At some point they were bitten by snakes because they quarreled with God. They perished in the desert, because they did not mix the promise with faith. No one can add one day to his or her life by complaining (Matthew 6:27).

When we complain instead of worshipping God, we quarantine our destinies, we delay our ways out of troubles. Worship instead will always make the problem very small. Worship will always create enough pressure to burst every limit to our success. Each time I live in the mode of worship, I find myself standing on ground that is higher than my problem. I have censored every complaining mode in my life.

My Testimony

Each time we are faced with challenges, we have a choice whether to praise and worship or to complain. It is entirely our choice, whether we trust God's Word over our problems or our situations over the promises of God.

When I was preparing for my examinations, I asked God to help me pass all my courses. I vowed that if He let me pass all of them, I would give myself to serve Him at my local church. Then in January of the flowing year I went to see (just to view) my result, since I could not receive hard copies as the result of an outstanding balance I owed to the university. Unfortunately, I had failed one course, thus contradicting the request I made to the Lord. I felt that I would not go back to enroll to repeat this course for another year. Instead of complaining, I said, "Thank you, God, for I know you make all things to work for my good." I was personalizing the Scripture in Romans 8:28.

If I were to go by the terms of my request, it would mean that I was not bound to serve God, because I failed. Instead I believed otherwise. I felt that because God was making all things work for my good, I might as well make my vows. I committed myself to the local church and introduced special days for prayer and fasting. I forgot about the failure. I worked as someone who had passed according to the terms. That year, while praying and fasting, a friend called me to come to the city to look for work. That was my first miracle. To make a long story short, I found myself working. But a big miracle was still to follow.

Called to Graduate

That year, around September, I called the university to check the date on which my friend was to graduate. The administrator asked for my student number instead of giving me a date. I gave her my student number anyway, and to my shock, the lady on other end of the phone said, "You are graduating," and she gave me the date for my graduation.

Unfortunately I was not prepared to go, but it meant I had passed all my courses, including the one I had failed. Immediately I called the course coordinator to tell him about the situation, and he said, "There is nothing I can do about it; good luck." You can imagine my goose bumps. My faith was lifted to another level. God is not a respecter of persons. If He did it to me, he can do it for you. Choose to praise and worship. It's a decision you can make, and it's up to you. Jesus is Lord and does not change. A decision to live a life of worship will turn your life around. There is a lifting up in worship.

CHAPTER 9

Worship in Spirit and in Truth

But the hour is coming, and now is, when true worshippers will worship the father **in spirit and truth, for the Father is seeking such to worship him.**
—John 4:23

For we are the circumcision who worship God in the Spirit, and have no confidence in the flesh ...
—Philippians 3:3

True worship is of the spirit; the Father seeks such worship. God gave birth to the spirit (John 3:6–8). I have seen many people trying to worship God intellectually (in the flesh). They often say few words, then stop and watch others worshipping God deeply in the spirit. When you worship in the spirit, you do not struggle to think of the right words. True worship happens when there is total harmony between the spirit of man and the Spirit of God. The Holy Spirit of God knows the mind and the will of God. The inner man is the one birthed by God (born again). God fellowships with the spirit, for the natural man cannot receive the things of the Spirit, as they are spiritually discerned. God primarily connects with the spirit. He is the Father of spirits, not of flesh.

Remember what the Bible says: "The spirit of a man is the kindle of the Lord" (Proverbs 20:27). We would not know God without revelation. We also therefore worship God based on revelation. (See 1 Corinthians 2:10–16). Knowing God by revelation is a spiritual phenomenon. Remember how John came about writing the book of Revelation? He was in the spirit and started to see things, and what a fellowship he had with the Godhead! When he saw Jesus, he bowed down. To bow down is to worship God.

Worship by Faith

Worship is an act of faith. It is impossible for any worship to please God unless it emanates from faith. The Bible is explicit in stating that anything that does not proceed from faith is sin. (See Romans 14:23.) We worship by conviction of the Spirit rather than merely performing a duty.

Worship Is Proactive. Moses worshipped God when He manifested Himself. He would react to seeing and hearing God coming in a cloud or in the form of fire, with thundering bolts. Then he would immediately bow down in awe to worship God. (See Hebrews 12:18–21 and Deuteronomy 9:18–19.) Moses was reactive to seeing, hearing, and feeling the presence of God.

Unlike Moses' worship, our worship is proactive. In our dispensation, we worship God by faith first, and then He manifests His glory. For example, when saints get together by faith, we just know He is there with us, because He said, **"For where two or three are gathered**

together in my name, I am there in the midst of them" (Matthew 18:20).

It is now our custom that when we worship, we often have a moment of silence to respect the presence of the Holy Spirit. One night when we did this, people started falling out of their chairs. They capsized as if someone were forcefully pushing them sideways. At the time, I was doing nothing myself except focusing on the presence of God. The whole room was filled with groaning—a deep level of intense communion with God.

Worship is proactive because of faith, for faith is the evidence of the presence of God, which is not seen. We look not at things that can be seen. (See 2 Corinthians 4:18.) Hebrews 11:1 says, "... it is the evidence of things not seen." We not only believe, but we know confidently, that whenever we meet in His name, He is there; thus we behave in a manner befitting His presence. By faith we declare He is the healer before we see the healing. We declare He never disappoints even though we go through trying circumstances. We do not declare this while hoping that He will change the situation. We do so because by faith we have evidence in the spirit realm of the things we are hoping for. It's just a matter of time before they manifest physically.

Indeed, true worship is by faith and faith is of the spirit. Without faith it is impossible to please God. (See Hebrews 11:6.) By faith we have the tangibility of the spiritual things. Worship is made more real by faith. Faith sees evidence in the spiritual realm.

Doubt misses God. Doubt will always counteract the efficacy of faith. One night while at her university, a young girl called another girl to the podium to demonstrate the presence of the Holy Spirit. She first asked the girl to give her a lovely hug—and what a nice and confident hug it was. She thanked the girl and said to her, "In same way you hugged me, please hug the Holy Spirit." The girl froze and did not know what to do, and then the girl crumpled and cried. Then the girl in charge said to the congregation, "This is how we miss God. Because we do not see Him, we often assume He is not here. It does not mean He is not here with you when you don't see Him."

God is present in us and around us. He is real in us. He said, "... Lo, I am with you always, even unto the end of the age" (Matthew 28:20). I will always talk with Him whether I sense His presence or not, and I will still be confident that He hears, because He is always with me. Whether we are asleep or awake, He is with us.

Knowing Your God

You worship what you do not know; **we know what we worship**, for salvation is of the Jew.
—John 4:22

It is impossible to worship God in truth if you do not know Him. What are you going to say to Him? What kind of image appears to you when you worship Him? To worship is to declare who God is, through words and in service. That is why the Lord Jesus said to the Samaritan woman that she and her nation worshipped what they didn't know. True worship can happen only when one has had a conviction of the realities of the visible and invisible qualities and the attributes of the Godhead.

Moses did not struggle in worshipping the God who always appeared to Him. Moses was not guessing. From the first day, God revealed Himself to Moses. So Moses truly knew his God. How possible is it that he lay prostrate for forty days and nights? Humanly speaking, it is impossible, isn't it? But that's what happens when God has manifested and you have recognized Him.

Not knowing God, on the other hand, explains why some people are not getting through in their prayers. They pray amiss for lack of revelation. Do you have a revelation of how God looks?

When Paul was in Athens, he discovered that they had many gods with altars bearing their names. But on a particular altar was written: "TO THE UNKNOWN GOD" (Acts 17:23). This made Paul realize that the people of Athens were very religious. He considered it to be improper to worship God without knowing Him. He then used it as an opportunity to preach the gospel of Jesus Christ unto them. As he continued, he said to them, "truly, these times of ignorance God has overlooked, but now commands all men everywhere to repent" (Acts 17:30).

This is happening all over the body of Christ in the whole world. The greatest calamity in life is not knowing the one true God, for everything else will be void and in vain. How does one worship a God he or she does not know? Unless God builds a house, they that build it build in vain.

As God said it, "my people perish for lack of knowledge" (Hosea 4:6). He said in the book of Isaiah 43:10, "... My servants who I have chosen that you may know and believe Me, and understand that I am He. Before Me there was no God formed, nor shall there be after Me."

He says that you may know Him and believe Him. This means that knowing must come first. By knowing God, faith develops. Then you can worship by faith. The more you worship, the more revelation you get, and then it becomes a cycle of worship and revelation. Revelation leads to better worship, and worship prompts more revelations.

Seeing the Invisible God

A true worshipper must know what God looks like, what He is

capable of, and the holiness of His deity, among other things. One may ask, but if you cannot see God, how can you know what He looks like? The first place to start is in the Bible. The Holy Scriptures offer a wealth of information on what God looks like. In fact, the only way to know God is to read the Scriptures that describe His Son, the Word (Jesus Christ).

The Bible says, **"He is the image of the invisible God, the first born over all creation"** (Colossians 1:15). The same expression is recorded in Hebrews 1:2–3, where it is written, "… Has in these last days spoken to us by His Son, whom He has appointed heir of all things, through whom also He made the worlds; **who being the brightness of His glory and the express image of His person …"**

When one of His disciples, Phillip, demanded that Jesus should show them the Father, He said to him, "Have I been with you so long, and yet you have not known Me, Phillip? **He who has seen Me has seen the Father**; so how can you say, show us the father?" (John 14:9).

What God Is Like

We have seen from the scriptures that God looks like Jesus. I was amazed to see how our Lord looks like currently, as He is in Heaven. Looks differently from the portraits often displayed on the walls of our church buildings and homes. Below let's describe some of His attributes according what the Bible has recorded:

Positioned above the Cherubim

When we say to God, "you are the Most High God (El Elyon)," we declare that He is above all living beings. Ezekiel 1:26 says, "And above the firmament over their(Cherubs') heads was a likeness of a throne in appearance of like sapphire stone; on the likeness of a throne was a likeness with appearance of a man high above it."

The throne of God is above the four living beings, to declare Him the most high God. He is exalted above the throne.

Figure Like That of Man

The Scripture above shows that He also looks like man. His figure is like that of a man. He has a waist, according to Ezekiel 1:27. In the New Testament, John saw Him as having white hair and a head of pure white. He also had eyes, though they were like lightning. His face was like the sun in its strength. He had feet, waist, and chest. (See Revelation 1:13–16). Remember, we are made in His own image.

He Is Fire

God does not just look like fire; He is the consuming fire. Ezekiel saw that from His waist upward He was like amber (the color of a live coal), and from his waist down He looked like a flame of fire. Though His figure is in the likeness of man, His substance is fire. This is also evident in Hebrews 12:29, which says, "for our God is the consuming fire." Though He has the figure of man, His substance is spiritual fire.

Jehovah, the More Infinite God

Oftentimes when I worship, I close my eyes and imagine the infinite size of God (God omnipresent).[6] Naturally speaking, the space is infinite, but I understand that He created it, for nothing was made except that was made by Him. (See John 1:3.) So I imagine how He fills the infinite space around the cosmos. The Bible says He fills all things. (See Ephesians 1:22.) David said, "Where can I go from Your Spirit, where can I flee from Your presence" (Psalm 139:7). Even more I imagine that the space is actually in Him. My God is bigger than the infinite space. I also imagine His infinity in terms of time. He not only has an immortal nature, but He brought time into existence. Before time was, He is. He is God, the Alpha and the Omega, the beginning and the end. (See Revelation 1:8.) His knowledge is infinite. His power is infinite. He is the everlasting God. God is infinite in every way. He is

---

6   See chapter 1, "The God of the Universe."

omnipresent, omniscient, omnipotent, and eternal. Oh, bless His holy name.

There is nothing more infinite than Jehovah. My God, Jehovah, is more than infinite, beyond comprehension.

Worship: A Matter of the Heart

> These people draw near to Me with their mouth, And honour me with their lips, but their heart is far from me. And in vain they worship Me, teachings doctrine the commandments of men.
>
> —Matthew 15:8–9

It is the language of our hearts that arouses the pleasure of God. True worship proceeds from the heart. God looks at the heart and not the outward appearance. (See 1 Samuel 16:7.) The word *heart* is also translated as "spirit" or "the inner man," which is the real man. Since God is Spirit, fellowship with Him must occur in the spirit. Worshipping God with the lips only, without the heart, is in vain. God seeks to be worshipped in Spirit. There always has to be complete congruence between the heart and the mouth. They that worship the Father must worship in Spirit, and in truth. (See John 4:23).

Worship is a matter of the heart. God looks at the heart more than what comes out of the mouth. In our main reference Scripture, Jesus says, "These people draw near to me with their mouth and honour me with their lips but the heart is far away from me."

The heart is the center of communion with God. To God, the voice of the heart is louder than that of the lips. There is no greater and more accurate divine vocabulary than that of the language of the heart. There is not a barrier to what the voice of the spirit can do. When we worship from our heart, we stir up the glory of God. If it's not from the heart, it is not worship but a religious ritual.

Spiritual Transaction

Imagine you are going to cross the border to a country in which they use a different currency. When you get to the border, you must convert the money you have so it will be useable in the country of your destiny. So is the mystery of prayer; it gets converted into the substance of heaven.

It is important to note that worship, just like prayer, is a spiritual transaction. In addition to the fact that we worship in the spirit, there is an amazing process that takes place in heaven. Our prayer expressions, or praise and worship, are converted from natural acts or languages into heavenly expressions of prayer. Our prayer reaches God not in English, Spanish, or any other human language. God receives our prayers as incense presented by archangels. Revelation 5:8 says, "Now when He had taken the scroll, the four living creatures ([i.e., cherubs]) and the twenty –four elders fell down before the lamb, each having a harp, and golden bowls full of incense, which are the prayers of the saints."

This means that when we pray in human language or verbally, our prayers get converted before reaching God. I call this a spiritual transaction.

The Groaning: Mortality Swallowed Up

> Likewise the Spirit also helps in our weaknesses. For we do not know what we should pray for as we ought, but the Spirit Himself makes intercession for us with **groaning which cannot be uttered.**
>
> —Romans 8:26

There is a language beyond human words and comprehension. That is the language of the recreated spirit. The recreated spirit is in union with the Holy Spirit of God. When we groan and sob, our prayers can permeate anything. This happens as we pray and our spirits cleave in prayer with the Holy Spirit, to declare mysteries incomprehensible to the natural mind. If we were to pray in the natural language, we would not know what to say. The Holy Spirit at the helm directs the supernatural prayer to change things.

One night I started praying, and before I knew it I started to worship God deeply in the Spirit. I started groaning in the spirit, and God inspired me to start praying for my sister-in-law, who was seriously sick. At that time the Holy Spirit knew what I should pray for and how to pray. I started calling her name, refuting the spirit of death, and appropriating the blood of the holy Lamb of God. I sobbed and groaned till about 0300 in the morning, when my wife was awakened by a cell phone ringing. She came to the lounge room where I was praying. She then gave me the mobile phone, and on the other end was my brother-in-law. He explained that something strange was happening with his sister (meaning my sister-in-law).

I discovered that while I was praying, she was dying. She could see dead people calling her to come, and her spirit was almost out. I asked them to put a phone to her ear, but unfortunately she could not hear me, as she was in another world. Instead of talking to me, she was talking to the spirit of death. I decided to rebuke that spirit, and she came back and started talking to me.

We order the course of events in the spirit realm. The Holy Spirit knows how to pray and what to pray for. When we groan, the Holy Spirit has taken over beyond our comprehension and we declare mysteries.

CHAPTER 10

Creating an Atmosphere of Worship

Worship is sacred and requires the right atmosphere. Yet it does not happen automatically. It requires a conscious decision and effort on the part of the worshipper. The responsibility to create such an atmosphere is ours, not God's.

I have often tried to worship God in the presence of my children. Oftentimes my last born (currently a toddler) would come and want me to pick him up and play with him. At times when I started to sob, he would be disturbed and would try to comfort me and try to wipe away my tears. As a result, my focus and concentration level were disturbed.

The virtues of total worship are communicable, such that every born-again Christian has an equal potential and opportunity to reach the deepest or highest level of communion with God. You can experience God through worship, but the onus is upon you. Let's go through some of the factors that will catapult a Christian to experience total worship. Whether we hinder or perpetuate worship depends on us, individually and corporately.

Cooperating with the Holy Spirit

But the helper, the Holy Spirit, who the Father will send in my name,
He will teach you all things …
—John 14:26

Likewise the Spirit also helps in our weaknesses. For we do not know
what we should pray for as we ought, but the Spirit Himself makes
intercession for us with groaning which can not be uttered.
—Romans 8:26

We can reach the ultimate worship only when we let the Holy Spirit of God be the captain of the procession. "… No one can say Jesus is Lord, except by the Holy Spirit" (1 Corinthians 12:3). It is by the Spirit that we cry, Abba Father. (See Romans 8:15.) He goes beyond the ability of the flesh in prayer. The accuracy of worship comes primarily by the Spirit of God. He gives us the right words and the ability to utter them. (See Acts 2:4.) Jesus offered Himself through the Holy Spirit, and by the same Spirit He offered His blood on the mercy seat. We also need the Holy Spirit to offer our lives and bodies as living sacrifices unto God. The perfection of worship is attained by the Spirit of God. He knows when and how to pray, when to groan, when to pray in other tongues, and when to pray with understanding. He leads us into the perfect will of God, for He knows the mind of God. He leads us into all the truth, and His word is truth. And they that worship Him must do so in Spirit and in truth.

Not cooperating with the Spirit of God can be costly. Without Him no one can ever reach the ultimate worship. Without the Spirit, we would lose out on what God is intending to do in our midst. The Holy Spirit knows the best way to worship; therefore He must be at the helm of our services. Jesus trusted Him to do this Job. He is the captain of the church. He is the captain of the armies of God. He must therefore take a lead in worship. If Jesus depended on Him at all levels of His life, who are we not to? We must follow the example of Jesus Christ.

We often have orderly and stringent service programs, yet the Master is left out of them. The Spirit is supposed to lead, but instead we often shut Him up. Many times one is prompted to start worshipping but ignores the prompt for one reason or the other. I have heard people say "I wanted to cry, but I stopped praying, for I thought of what people would think of me." There must be a point of surrender; a point at which we allow Him to lead. It was the Holy Spirit prompting you to pray in the Spirit language. There is no better timing than that of the Spirit. I often went to service with a powerful message but left without preaching it because the Holy Spirit led us into worship. Everyone left those services highly fulfilled. Some were even healed. Others received prophetic messages that changed lives. I have often seen people hinder the movement of the Spirit.

The Spirit of God is God with us. God relates to us through His Spirit. God is that Spirit. The Holy Spirit is the one who helps us in our infirmities. He lifts our prayers above natural language. Whenever He prompts us, we must follow suit. We often fall into the temptation of quenching the Spirit of God by ignoring His leading. This often happens because we endeavor to be professional in managing our time, which is a good thing, of course. As a result, we keep stringent schedules in which even the Holy Spirit is denied time.

Though we must strive to be orderly and professional, the Holy Spirit must always have the last say. We can prepare programs, but the Spirit must have a last say.

Consecration

> Pursue peace with all people and **holiness** without
> which it is impossible to see God.
> —Hebrews 12:14

In the Old Testament, the high priest needed consecration before entering the holiest place; otherwise, he would not come back alive. Consecration is the process by which we are made holy; the word *consecration* is often used interchangeably with the word *sanctification*. Holiness is a fundamental of worship. Holiness refers to being set apart for a special purpose in righteousness. The Bible says, "... He chose us in Him before the foundation of the world, that we should be holy and without blame in love"(Ephesians 1:4). We come into the presence of God with the consciousness that we are a holy generation and a royal priesthood. We stand in the consciousness of righteousness of God, without condemnation in our hearts, in Christ.

We come to God with total commitment and dedication. We know that He is our life, our breath, and our substance and that without Him we can't live. Ours is a life of sacrifice to God. We understand that we are set apart for God. Our consciences do not accuse us, so we cannot be judged. As such, we yield our bodies and souls to no other, but only God. Yielding our lives to another would be defilement. Yielding to another is like being corrupted with a virus that interrupts the perfect fellowship with God. We are free from corruption in Christ Jesus.

We are now qualified to participate in the divine nature of God and in the heritage of the saints. The Bible also says, *"Be ye Holy as I Am holy"* (I Peter 1:16). In the Old Testament they would perform rituals to consecrate the Levites and priests before ministering to the Lord. (See Leviticus 8.) In the New Testament, our consecration is different from the old. In the New Testament, Jesus says we are consecrated (sanctified) by the word of God. (See John 17:17). The word of God consecrates us as we conform to it. We have no guilty conscience. When Paul wrote to Timothy, he said, "Now the purpose of the commandment is love from a **pure heart, from a good conscience, and from a sincere faith** ..." (I Timothy 1:5).

When you are set apart unto God for to serve Him, it specifically means that you are made pure and free from the sin of worshipping other gods. God summarized these facts very nicely to Moses in Leviticus 20:1–8:

> Then the Lord spoke to Moses, saying, "Again, you shall say to the children of Israel: 'However of the

children of Israel, or of the strangers who dwell in Israel, who gives any of his descendants to Molech, He shall surely be put to death. The people of the land shall stone him with stones. I set my face against and will cut him off form his people because he has given some of his descendant to Molech, to defile My sanctuary and profane My Holy name ..., Consecrate yourselves therefore, and be holy, for am the Lord your God ... , I am the Lord who sanctifies you.'"

The Power of Total Surrender

... God resist the proud and, but gives grace to the humble. Therefore submit to God. Resist the devil and he will flee from you ... Humble yourselves in the sight of the Lord, and He will lift you up.

—James 4:6–10

Total surrender is the essence of true worship. No worship can be in truth until one has reached a point of total surrender. A true servant submits his own will to that of his master. The servant lives to please the master in every way possible. When we consciously decrease and He increases, that's a point of surrender. (See John 3:30.) Yet in our case, the more we decrease, the higher we are lifted up. Because when we exalt Him, we will find ourselves in Him. Where He is, there we are, because we are in Him. True worship is more effective when we have unconditionally surrendered all to Jesus, withholding nothing. That's what Abraham did. He trusted in God that he could give his only beloved son, and trusted that God would raise Isaac up from the dead. (See Hebrews 11:17–19.)

Trusting means leaning on God and not on our own understanding. This is the reason others are not fully surrendered to God—lack of trust. Most people who can't worship God with their tithes cannot worship because they can't fully trust God to be their provider. There is nothing we cannot give to God. In surrendering, we shift our trust from flesh to total trust in God. Paul surrendered everything for the sake of knowing Christ (Philippians 2:4–8). Everything must be laid at the cross. That's when we become conscious that our lives have been crucified with Christ. Unless a corn of wheat falls and dies, it remains alone. (See John 12:24.) Our worship will never rise beyond the level of our humility. Whatever we lose for Christ's sake we gain a hundred times more here on earth or in this life. (See Mark 10:29–30).

Surrendering Your Own Glory

Another excellent example of surrender in worship is in the book of John 12:3: "Then Mary took a pound of very costly oil of spikenard, anointed the feet of Jesus, and wiped His feet with her hair. And the house was filled with the fragrance of the oil."

According to the estimation of Judas, the oil could have been sold for three hundred denarii. According to the footnotes of some Bibles, the amount was equivalent to the annual wage of an average earner. This helps us understand how much she surrendered because of the revelation she had of Christ.

As if that were not enough, she bowed down to wipe Jesus' feet with her own hair. Just imagine that! A lady's hair is her crown of glory. I imagine that Jesus' feet were dusty, but she bowed down below His knees and wiped the oily dust from His feet. That speaks volumes. Most people won't even bow down because of the expensive designer suits they wear. But those who know Christ—they surrender all and know He will bring them more suits in this life. In true worship, we surrender all from the heart and are fulfilled beyond measure.

The Power That Exalts

The power of exaltation is in surrendering. When we humble ourselves in the sight of the mighty God, we are lifted up.

Finally, let's look at what Paul said about the humility of Christ in Philippians 2:3–11:

Let nothing be done through selfish ambition or conceit, but in lowliness of mind let each esteem others better than himself. Let each of you look out not only for his own interests, but also for the interests of others. Let this mind be in you which was in Christ Jesus, who being in the form of God, did not consider it robbery to be equal with God, but made Himself of **no reputation**, taking the form of **a bondservant**, coming in the likeness of men. And being found in the appearance as man, **He humbled Himself and became obedient** to the **point of death**, even the death of the cross. Therefore **God also highly exalted Him** and given Him a name which is above every name, that at the name of Jesus every knee should bow, of those in heaven and those on earth, and that every tongue should confess that Jesus Christ is Lord, **to the glory of God the Father.**

Surrendering to God is like a seed; when thrown down and buried in the soil, it sprouts out in the newness of glory. This explains the power of the principle of sowing seeds and reaping. A seed buried in the ground receives a new nature and the power to increase (grows and multiplies). Christ humbled Himself so that God would be able to exalt Him. He then received a glorified body and a name above every other name. This is where most people fail. They intentionally and arrogantly become stubborn in the presence of God. They can't submit a thing to God, yet they want what only God can give them.

They way up is the way down. When we humble ourselves, we get lifted by a higher power. When we surrender our best, He automatically takes away our worst; infirmities and mortality are swallowed up. Our weaknesses, bitterness, fears, hatred, and all the infirmities of our faculties are consumed. We get upheld by the right hand of power and start hailing from the top.

Most people miss God by being stuck in the flesh. We must mortify the transactions of the flesh, and then the life of the Spirit will be truly manifested in us. You must swallow your pride lest you miss the greatest thing that could happen to men. A place of surrender is our point of exaltation. His glory operates in us to His own glory. Amen! Hallelujah!

The Power of Reverence

> Therefore since we are receiving a kingdom which can not be shaken, let us have grace, by which we may serve God acceptably with reverence and godly fear. For our god is a consuming fire.
>
> —Hebrews 12:28–29

Those who fear God will fearlessly stand against any force. Worship must be full of reverence. Reverence refers to the fear of God in respect of His deity. And as it is written, "the fear of the Lord is beginning of wisdom: but fools despise wisdom and instruction" (Proverbs 1:7). If people could worship idols, which were made with human hands, with reverence, how much more reverence could they give to the one true living God? Surely He deserves better. They that fear Him will always obey and live in fully sundered lives, serving Him. They will always be set apart from the rest because they serve God. God will always hear those who fear Him. The Bible says,

> Then those who feared the Lord spoke to one another and, and the Lord listened and heard them; so a book of remembrance was written before Him, for those who fear the Lord and who meditate on His name ... "And I will spare them as a man spares his own son who serves him. Then you shall again discern between the righteous and the wicked, between one who serves God and one who does not serve Him." (Malachi 3:16–18)

The Word Factor

The Word of God must be treated with absolute reverence and confidence. *The Word of God holds the whole integrity of God.* The Word is God Himself. Thus, the reverence and the confidence put on the Word must be the same as put on His voice or word of prophecy. (See Hebrews 4:7.) Therefore, the Word must be the foundation of worship. He has exalted His Word above His entire name. (See Psalm 138:2.)

Praying through the Word

There is no better way of communicating with God than through the language of His own Word. The Word is the voice of the Holy Spirit penned down in ink. Worship has everything to do with the Word. One can't worship except through the Word. The Word is Spirit and the life of God. The Word of God directs our worship, for the living Word is the rock upon which our faith is founded. Without faith, we can't worship God in truth; as such, we will not be able to please Him indeed. The kingdom of God is of words. We were saved because of the engrafted Word (James 1:21). The world was created by the word. Worship is by faith and faith comes by hearing the Word. The Word is also the foundation of our attitudes and thought patterns, toward both God and the world around us.

When we think and pray through the Word, we will always please God. The Word defines us. It is the same Word that discerns our thoughts and the intents of our hearts. (See Hebrews 4:12.) The same Word also consecrates our hearts. (See Psalm 119:8.) Thus we stand in His presence without guilt, and worship with confidence and boldness of faith.

The Shouting Point

As I said earlier, it is easy for most people to start worshipping and shouting when they see a miracle. The integrity of the Word of God is a good reason, enough for us to start praising God even before we see a miracle. The Word of God is dependable and infallible. It is

God speaking to us. The Word endures forever. (See Mark 13:31.) The Word is able to save us. (See James 1: 21.) So we can sign our lives on the Word of God. Our lives hang on this same Word. The Word of God is enough to get us shouting in the face of impending doom. It is a good enough reason to get us worshipping God, because He watches His Word to fulfill it.

This is the story of King Jehoshaphat, in the book of 2 Chronicles 20:15–19. When he heard that the mighty army of the Enemy was coming against him, he was afraid. He then humbly beseeched the Lord to help. Most interesting is that instead of God doing directly what he asked for, God sent forth the Word through the mouth of the prophet Jehaziel. The prophet said, "... do not be afraid nor be dismayed because the battle is not yours, but God's ... , you will not need to fight in this battle. Position yourselves, stand still and see the salvation of the Lord, who is with you, oh Judah and Jerusalem ... **And Jehoshaphat bowed his head with his face to the ground, and all Judah and the inhabitants of Jerusalem bowed before the Lord and worshipped.**"

When King Jehoshaphat heard these words, he was driven to start worshipping God. You will realize that after these words, the Enemy was still evidently pursuing them. The Enemy was still out there, intending to conquer Judah and Jerusalem. Yet for the king, the Word of God was enough for him to start shouting for victory.

The Bible shows that after the king heard the word of prophecy through the mouth of the prophet, he was convinced that there was no way other than God's way. Because of his confidence in the word of God, fear was smitten; worry was thrust out of his heart, and instead he was provoked into worship. He bowed down on his face and worshipped the Lord, God of the armies of Israel. He could smell victory.

For most people, the Word is not yet enough. They want the word to be proven first; then they will worship. It is after they have seen that they can finally believe that the case is settled. The power of worship lies in the fact that we understand that the Word of God carries the substance of our needs and has final authority in our lives. We have more confidence in our God than in our enemies. Our Enemy is a mere mortal, Satan, and our God is immortal. The Devil himself fears the man who carries the revelation of the word. True worshippers know the true value of the Word in worship. The moment you receive the Word—either through the Bible, by prophecy, or through whatever channel God chooses to use—you have a reason to start shouting. The Word of God is the answer you were looking for. Yet the battle is not yet over; you still need to act to convert your miracle into material substance.

Fellowship with the Word

Always when you read the Word, you are fellowshipping with God. The Bible shows that in the beginning the word was God. Revelation 19:13 also shows that His name is the Word of God. The Word is a living person. The word proceeds from the Father. Though the Word was written thousands of years back, it is still fresh. The Word is alive now. When we read and meditate on the Word, we receive life.

The Word also improves our relationship with God. Your obedience to the Word becomes worship. Your worship will always get God's attention. They that worship Him must worship in Spirit and in truth (See John 4:23.) The Word is Spirit. (See John 6:63.) They that worship Him in Spirit find that the Word is truth. (See John 17:17.) They that worship Him must worship in truth. The Word undoubtedly creates an atmosphere of praise and worship to those who have complete reverence and confidence.

The moment we receive the word for our situation, whether written or spoken, it must be a shouting point. We can often receive the word through prophecy, through the written word, or by illumination in our spirits. While praying, the Spirit can remind you of a Scripture or can give you direct instructions that will get you out of your situation. Honoring the Word will ensure the results. We begin to celebrate our answers from God. The Word of God is as good as done.

The Shouting Point Is Proof of Faith

Celebrating God in the face of storms shows that we have complete confidence in the integrity of the word. Oftentimes it is accompanied by acting on the word as if it is already done. It might require that we obey the word and start worshipping God not only through the sacrifices of our lips but also by bringing a material sacrifice as proof of our faith. True worship is the proof of our faith in God.

Prayer of Declaration

I used to share a room with a man by the name of Nigel Mokhwaripa, who is now a pastor of Maranatha Church International, Soweto branch. By God's grace he happened to be my mentor in most areas. He is a man of faith, given to the Word and prayer. Oftentimes he would wake up at 0400 to pray until 0800. In his prayer, he would not petition anything. He would instead thank God, praising Him for His faithfulness. He would declare only that what the Word of God says is true in his own life.

I would witness God promoting Him miraculously. He would say, "God, I thank you, because I know I am the head and not the tail." I saw God working miracles in his life. God promoted him miraculously within a short space of time. It was through this kind of prayer that God healed members of his family. When members of his family were attacked by demonic forces, he challenged other family members not to take them to witch doctors, stating that if God did not deliver them, then they could take them wherever they wanted. Guess what—there were no two ways about it. He delivered his family from apparent vicious demonic attacks of mental oppression. Yet the man only praised and worshipped by declaring Him through the Holy Scriptures.

Remote Effect

At one time while Pastor Nigel Mokhwaripa was still a teenager, he was led by the Spirit to worship and praise in song while declaring to everyone in the streets the good news of the kingdom of God. While he was busy doing that, there was an aura of glory that filled his church. On that day, all the people attending the service where dumb until he stopped. Not even one person could speak. This is the power of true praise and worship. There is a nature in us that can lie dormant unless we stir it up. Worship stirs up the godly nature in us, such that from a distance we are able to affect situations. Because of the aura of the glory, we are able to affect things remotely as if we were there in flesh.

In declaration, the spirit gets a hold of a thing and does not let go, and it materializes. The boldness of declaration is made by confidence in the word, knowing the word has power to birth what we declare. When you believe in the power of the Word, you shall declare a thing and it shall be established for you. (See Job 22:28.) In this case, declaration is arrived at by confessing the Word.

Imagination in Worship

I never try to worship without pictorial meditation. I imagine and meditate deeply on the image of God as laid out by the Word. I close my eyes, and I can clearly see Jesus being lifted above the cherubim, white hair, face shining, a two-edged sword issuing from His mouth, thunderbolts crashing, fire and lightning flashing, a river of many waters flowing, and so on. I see the God who fills the universe, the cosmos, and the infinite firmament. My God is big. That's what I imagine when I say, "You are big."

I also imagine His works of power—how He parted the Red Sea, how quail and manna fell form heaven, how He made the rock gush out enough water for millions of souls and their flocks. I imagine His glory covering the tabernacle, the pillar of fire, and the river of fire from the throne and cloud. This is awesome. My God is real.

The Faith Factor[7]

Without faith, it is impossible to please God. (See Hebrews 11:6.) True worship must arouse God's pleasure. That which is not of faith is sin. (See Romans 14:23.) We know not how to worship except by faith.

---

[7]   See Chapter 10, point 1: Worship by Faith

God is Spirit and can only be worshipped in Spirit. Only by faith can we operate in the spiritual realm. It is by faith that we know He is the one true God. Faith touches the concreteness of the spiritual realm. Faith touches and feels the depth of God. Faith is like a bridge by which we enter the Holy of Holies.

Practicing the Presence of God

Faith is more concrete than imagination. Though imagination ushers one into realizing the presence, faith is the evidence of the actual presence of the unseen God. By faith we plunge into God and start doing things to God, who is present with us. I have heard stories of people who set up two chairs—one for the worshipper and one for God. They conclude that God is sitting on the other chair by faith, and they start a conversation with God.

"I Had No Choice but to Hire You"

A good example of such practice is a woman who preached on a Women's Day special service in our church. She testified that she set up a chair for Jesus and told Him that she needed a job. Soon after that she received a prophecy to specifically go to a particular bank the following Monday. She woke up on Monday by faith and headed to the taxi stand. At the taxi stand she found that the last seat was reserved for her. When the taxi was going past the bank, surprisingly the taxi driver said to her, "Get out here; the bank you are looking for is there," pointing to the direction of the bank. Upon getting out of the taxi, she found a person waiting for her who said, "We have been waiting for you."

She was led to the reception area and then to the interview room. Then she got the job just like that. Surprisingly, she was not qualified for it. Later she was shocked by the report of the person who was leading the interviews. She told her that while interviewing her, there was a terrible voice that continually said, "Hire this lady! Hire this lady! You will hire this lady!" The lady said, in retrospect, "I had no choice but to hire you." She realized that all that happened on that day was the ministry of the angels charged upon her life by God. Yet it didn't just happen. It was an initiative on the side of the worshipper.

It all started with understanding the presence of God and taking advantage of it. It is a practice every worshipper can engage in. This is active faith, which is able to catapult one above plain human logic. The heavens will always get together for the one who exercises such faith.

Worshipping God requires us to actively exercise this kind of faith by acknowledging God's presence. As I said before, we often ask the congregation to keep silent to honor the presence of the Holy Spirit in our midst, the results of which are always tremendous. Oftentimes people fall down without anyone touching them and without anyone commanding it to happen. People who visit with us often report that they have never seen such kind of worship. Moses always fell prostrate at the sight of God. In our dispensation, we practice the presence by faith first, knowing that God's presence will manifest as a result. We walk not by sight but by faith.

Unity in Fellowship

> And the glory which you gave me I have given to them, **that they may be one just as We are one:** I in them, and you in Me; that they may be made perfect in one, and that they That they may be made perfect in one, and that the world may know that You have sent me, and have loved Me.
>
> —John 17:22–23

Unity in the church is never optional. It is mandatory if we are to see and experience the power of worship. Jesus took His time to pray to the Father that we may be one (united). This must have been important to Jesus. Have you ever wondered why He was so concerned about unity? Because we are one body—the body of Jesus Christ—so we can't operate in disunity. The early church discovered this; they were of one mind and spirit. They shared everything they had, that those who lacked had enough. Unity is the bond of love. Faith works by love. (See Galatians 5:6.) If we live in disunity, we live against the body. Many churches have scattered because of selfish ambitions. No individual can be bigger than the body. Let no one peruse selfish ambition, and God will be really glorified. The church must walk in agreement and in unity of faith.

Have you ever wondered why Paul spoke about the condemnation of not discerning the body? He said in of 1 Corinthians 11:29, "For he who eats and drinking an unworthy manner eats and drinks judgement to himself, not discerning the Lord's body. For this reason many are weak and sick among you, and many sleep."

Paul says here that judgment comes upon people who drink unworthily by not discerning the body of the Lord. In addition to the bread, the church (believers together) is the body of Christ. Paul said this because people selfishly rushed to eat and drink without considering others. Remember that "communion" means "fellowship" or "sharing together." Worship is therefore the deepest level of communion. Unity is therefore the perfect grounds for fellowship with God. If we are one body then, we must be knit together by love. We put one another first because whatever we do to another Christian, we are actually doing to Christ. (See Matthew 25:34–46.) Whenever we ignore the interests of others, we are ignoring Christ.

Most Christians are hypocrites. They come to church wearing a holy mask while their hearts hold grudges, competing for positions and imagining vain things. This is the reason some people will not be healed until they forgive others. Have fellowship in others' sufferings and pains, and do something about it. That way you will be fellowshipping with Christ Jesus. And our God is not unfaithful; He will not forget your works and labor of love that you have shown toward His name. (See Hebrews 6:10.)

Focus on God, not on the Situation

In order for the worshipper to create an atmosphere conducive for worship, one needs to shut the world out and focus on God, who is able to change situation. God is permanent, and your situation is temporal. When it comes to faith matters, you believe either God or your situation. Whomever your focus is on is whom you will magnify. It's either God or your situation that seems big to you. Do you not know that the one to whom you present yourself as a slave is the one whom you obey? (See Romans 6:16.)

Your focus will determine who will prevail in your life. When one focuses on the troubles he or she is facing, he or she is likely to believe the problems' impending destruction other than what the Word says regarding such a situation. Once you believe the problem and believe in the invincibility of the problem, you will confess it. That which you confess, you possess. Every problem that appears to be a mountain before you shall disappear—not by your own strength, but by the Spirit of the mighty God. (See Zechariah 4:7–9.)

The Right Spot: Alone with God

So He Himself often withdrew into the wilderness and prayed.

—Luke 5:16

Now it came to pass in those days that He went out to the mountain to pray, and continued all night in prayer to God.

—Luke 6:12

Jesus often left the multitudes, including His own inner circle of three—Peter, James, and John—to pray alone in a deserted place. He sometimes had overnight prayers alone with God. There is a need to be alone with God more often where you are not cluttered by the things of the world or where there are not many voices. He wanted to clearly hear the voice of God without disturbances. The same was done by Moses; he left the multitudes to meet God either at the mountain or the tabernacle.

You must remove any obstacles that would impede on your focused worship. Shut yourself off from the outside world so you can focus on God. We are living in a busy and noisy world, such that we are disturbed left and right. Sometimes while you are deep in fellowship, a phone rings; often it becomes impossible to return to the same level of fellowship. Sometimes you have uninvited guests. This happened to me many times, and I was disturbed. It is safe to suggest that one should even leave the house and go to a special spot where he or she will not be tempted to put things in order.

True worship requires some quiet time with God. I often prefer to close my eyes when I worship God. I shut my mind off from my problems and my surroundings, and focus on the revealed image, attributes, and glory of God according to the Word. Genuine worship is possible only when we focus on God.

I remember when this truth dawned on me. I was still at university, just after I just saw the lightning and came to understand how big or great God is as compared to the earth, moon, sun, stars, and other planets. I joined the prayer at 10:00 p.m., and when it was time to pray, I hid under a desk. Instead of petitioning, I imagined how great God was and started confessing these words: "You are greater than the earth I am standing on; You are bigger than my mind can imagine. You are sovereign and absolute in power. You are bigger than my enemies and my problems. Therefore I will not be confounded."

Each time I would do these; my situation would change within a short space of time. I understood that in fact I was at the helm of things. I stood on higher ground. I could postpone a due date for assignments through praise and worship. As somebody said, "He who bows before God can stand before any man."

Each time I close my eyes, I see Jesus on the throne, with a sword in

His mouth. His robe is dipped in blood, with a sash of gold, His face shining like the sun at full strength, and His feet like bronze coming out of a furnace. When worshipping, I want to see God, not people. I imagine thunderbolts and lightning coming from that throne lifted above the cherubim. When I do this, a tense emotion of true worship fills my soul and I worship in truth and in Spirit. Opening my eyes could make me lose focus.

At times you might need to leave your home and go somewhere quieter, where you know you will not be disturbed by children, a life partner, or common domestic activities. Sometimes fasting might mean you shut off your television and cell phone for a time. This is to give God perfect attention without any hindrances.

The Role of Music in Worship

> And do not be drunk with wine in which is dissipation, but be filled with the Spirit, speaking to another **in psalms and hymns and spiritual songs, singing and making melodies in pure heart to the Lord**, giving thanks always for all things to God the father, in the name of our Lord Jesus Christ, submitting one to another in the fear of God.
>
> —Ephesians 5:18–20

Music is one of the most effective tools in creating an atmosphere of worship. The right song at the right time will definitely usher us into the highest possible level of communion with God. I have discovered that even some good secular songs can get you crying. This is indicative of the inherent power of music. If secular music can affect people so deeply, then how much truer is this for a spiritual song? It will not only affect your soul but will also reach even to the throne room of God, through our hearts. According to the above Scripture, the Bible instructs us to sing and make melodies in pure heart to the Lord.

This was evidently the case with Jehoshaphat. The Bible shows that after having consulted with the leaders, he appointed singers to sing unto the Lord and praise His beauty as they went before the army. When they began to sing and to praise, the Lord set ambushes against the people of Ammon, Moab, and Mount Seir, and He utterly defeated them in favor of the Jews (2 Chronicles 20:21–22).

We also see from the Bible that most prophets needed music to create an atmosphere for prophesies. For example, when Elisha wanted to hear from the Lord, he called for a musician. And when the musician played, the hand of the Lord was upon him and he started prophesying. (See 2 Kings 3:15–19.) Here we see a voluntary initiative to plunge into the realm of divine intervention. God gave victory.

Everything Looked Small

One night while at university, I took my CD player and my favorite worship songs to a classroom. Alone I prayed nonstop from 0000 till dawn. That is the power of song. I sang unto God, encouraging my soul with the same songs. When I started singing, more and more revelations came to my spirit and ushered me into unstoppable worship. By the time I left that class, it felt as if the earth were a small thing. I was elevated by the presence of God. People around me looked small. Because I had been in communion with such a great God, everything else looked small. It was a tremendous experience I had as a young Christian. Music is able to stir our souls and hearts into worship.

Indeed, music will always play a major role in praise and worship. We often sing when we are happy to celebrate, and when we are feeling down to lift us up. Music is often an irresistible force that can usher one into utter worship. Universally, music has gone beyond entertainment. It is more like religion to many. It seems we cannot live without it. Music has gone viral throughout the world. Evidently, music has inherent power over the soul and heart of man.

God loves music. He loved it long before we knew there was something called music. Lucifer was a great singer in the presence of God. (See Isaiah 14:11.) Angels are singing before the throne of God. (See Revelation 14:3.) God receives pleasure from music.

The power of music in worship cannot be denied. There is glory that manifests while we worship in song. We see demons cry and leave people while we worship. Remember David playing a harp for King Saul. People get healed and miracles take place during worship songs. Once during a main service I took the microphone and started to worship in song. One of the brothers jumped high while shouting, and he fell down. The glory of he Lord was upon Him, and it was difficult for him to even stand up. On another occasion I lay flat on the floor and started a song. People started falling, and some time later a brother told me that he saw fire on me. On several occasions there were reports of fire around me when I facilitated worship. There are testimonies of people who were healed by this kind of worship.

My wife also told me a powerful story. Apparently they had a youthful congregation in a rural village of Limpopo Province, South Africa. Some rebellious youths who stood against the church started throwing stones on the roof of the building they were using for services. Realizing they had nothing to fight back with, the youthful congregation started singing a song unto God. The results were that the Holy Spirit started bringing the attackers into the church service one by one. They humbled themselves and repented. That's the power of worship. It allows God to fight for us. More often than not, instead of trying to be physically aggressive to demons, we would focus on praising and worshipping God and they would leave. They can't stand the atmosphere of worship. Music propels us to greater levels of worship.

Worship Songs Must Be Scriptural

It is very important to note that what we call worship or praise songs must always be scriptural. I have often encountered songs deemed worship songs that turned out to be unscriptural. Whenever I encounter such songs, I do not sing along, because I cannot agree with something against the Word of God. Our songs must always agree with the Word of Life and must be from the convicted heart.

Conclusion

Worship plunges you into the supernatural realm of God. Worshippers are powered by God. It is through worship that we bask and swim in the fullness of the life of God. The life of worship is the life of victory in Christ. Whether we are in good times or in trying times, we live in the mode of worship. The acts of worship activate the eternal power of God that has been lying dormant in us, so we must always initiate them in faith. The life of a believer, therefore, should never be void of worship. It is a continuous, active life in the realm of the Spirit. Total worship is life fulfilled in its totality, for we are primarily designed to be worshippers.

Prayer of Salvation

Are you born again? In order to worship in Spirit and in truth, you need to be born again. The Bible says, "... unless one is born again, he can not see the kingdom of God ... unless one is born of water and the Spirit, he cannot enter the kingdom of God" (John 3:3–5).

How Do You Become Born Again?

The Bible says, "... if you confess with your mouth the Lord Jesus and believe in your heart that God has raised Him from the dead you will be saved" (Romans 10:9). Therefore, if you believe and want to accept Christ as your Lord and Savior, pray this prayer:

> Dear God, I believe that Jesus is the Christ. He came in flesh and suffered in my place. I believe that you raised Him from the dead. Forgive all my sins and make me whole through the blood of your lamb. Make me your child today. Come and live in me and have all of me. Thank you, Father, for I am now born again. I am your child now. I receive your grace and mercy in the name of Jesus.

Congratulations. You are now a child of God, the Creator of the heaven and the earth. Have a personal communion with Him, study the Word, and pray always.

Now that you are born again, look for a church near you where they preach and demonstrate the full gospel of Jesus Christ. Endeavor to be baptized in the Holy Spirit. Testify to others about your experience of receiving Christ. Participate in fellowship meetings and other activities. Abraham's blessings are yours. Hallelujah!